EMPIRE BUILDER
Sam Brannan

Born: March 6, 1819
Died: May 5, 1889

There are men who in their personalities and careers seem to embody the vital spirit of their age. Such was Sam Brannan. In the era of the final great thrust westward to the Pacific, the discovery of gold, and the vast speculations that saw huge fortunes swiftly gained and lost, Sam Brannan stood out as one of the most daring of the breed of rugged individualists who set their mark so vividly upon the West. His is the story of a man who became a living legend as one of California's first great empire builders, a supreme gambler who knew both triumph and disaster—but never the meaning of fear.

Books by Bob and Jan Young

EMPIRE BUILDER

Sam Brannan

by Bob and Jan Young

Julian Messner · New York

Published simultaneously in the United States and Canada
by Julian Messner, a division of Simon & Schuster, Inc.,
1 West 39 Street, New York, N.Y. 10018. All rights reserved.
Copyright, ©, 1967 by Bob and Jan Young

Printed in the United States of America

Library of Congress Catalog Card No. 67-21615

FOR . . .
    BOB V. SMITH
    . . . WHO KNOWS WHY

Contents

1 Find a Thread

A skein of ducks flapped across the icy dawn sky on their way to a more hospitable situation. Far below, fourteen-year-old Sam Brannan strode resolutely down the rickety steps of the gaunt Maine farmhouse on his way to what he hoped was a better situation, too. A suspicious moisture clouded his eyes, but his mouth was grim as he crunched along the icy street from his parents' home to that of his sister Mary Ann and her husband, Alex Badlam.

Mary Ann, thirteen years older than Sam, had always treated her young brothers more like a second mother than an elder sister. Now that she and her new husband were moving to Painesville, Ohio, Sam had decided to go with her. He was bound to leave home soon, anyway. John, one older brother, had already run away to sea, and his other brothers, Tom and Dan, were planning to leave before long.

Old Tom Brannan, with his temper and his drinking, was the cause of his sons' unhappiness. Sam's father had come to America from Eire in 1775 when he was twenty, traveling steerage. Unskilled but a good worker, he found work first around Portland, Maine, then later moved to Saco, where he met and married Mary Goodrich. She died in 1805, grieving for their two sons who had died earlier, one of yellow fever and the other by drowning. A single daughter, Nancy, soon married and disappeared from the family records.

The conservative residents of Saco were a bit startled when Tom Brannan courted and married Sarah Emery only a few weeks after his first wife's death. Sarah was a handsome young woman whose dowry enabled them to purchase a substantial farm. Tom was fifty, eighteen years older than his bride, and his habits were well established. He preferred the warm fellowship of other middle-aged companions to the hard work of the farm or the demands of a new wife, his interest in home brightened only momentarily by the birth of their first child, Mary Ann, on July 4, 1806, and the four boys who followed: John, Tom, Dan and Samuel. He paid little attention to the children and became increasingly churlish as old age seeped into his joints and disposition.

Mrs. Brannan was a well-meaning but somewhat inadequate woman accustomed to being waited upon herself; and thus it fell to Mary Ann to look after the youngsters, particularly her favorite, Sam, who was born March 6, 1819.

Mary Ann proved such an efficient help to her parents that she had given up hope of ever becoming a bride until, when she was twenty-seven, Alexander Badlam, a clerk in the Saco mercantile store, came courting. They married quickly and made immediate plans to leave Saco to build their future farther west. Anxious to try the frontier, they chose a burgeoning area near the shores of Lake Erie in Ohio called Painesville. Their decision to pack a wagon and head west came about the same time that Sam received what he decided would be his last caning at the hands of his father, who too frequently implemented his rages with strong Irish whiskey.

Sam's most difficult job had been telling his mother. As he slammed the gate behind him and strode down the street toward the Badlams, he tried to forget the pain in her eyes and remember only her voice saying that she understood and was giving him her blessing.

Fortunately, Sam's strong hands, ready humor and quick mind made a welcome addition to the Badlams' household as they moved west. "Where's the Indians? Where's the frontier?" he asked eagerly once they reached Painesville. "This ain't nothin' but another Maine town. Gosh."

Mary Ann laughed at his disappointment. "Don't worry. Smart as you are, you'll find plenty to do without any Indians."

She was right. Before the neighbors had pitched in to help the Badlams with a house and barn raising, Sam already had found work as an apprentice to the Painesville *Press.* He was jubilant about the job. "I'll learn to be a printer, then I'll learn to write. Before long I'll own a newspaper myself," he bragged with new self-importance.

Mary Ann smiled. "Lands, Sam. You find a broken thread and you imagine a brocaded coat. You're a caution."

Because he wouldn't receive any wages for the length of his four-year apprenticeship, Sam continued to do chores for the Badlams for his room and board. Alex was an equally energetic worker, and it wasn't long before they were selling surplus crops to town folks and travelers. If it wasn't a bountiful living, at least they were happy and content, particularly when their first son, Alex Jr., was born. Sam was indulgent and spoiled his young nephew outrageously, and the parents and youthful uncle were even more pleased when Sarah was born a couple of years later in 1837.

By now the Badlams had become interested in the events going on at nearby Kirtland, where a dynamic personality, Joseph Smith, was preaching the doctrine of the Church of the Latter Day Saints to a new religious sect, the Mormons. The Badlams enjoyed these church activities and Sam frequently accompanied them, showing a teen-ager's interest in the freshly scrubbed young girls who attended the social and church functions. Since he liked to hint that he was really a reporter for the Painesville *Press* instead of a mere apprentice printer, he enjoyed considerable attention. After all, he reassured himself, he had just scraped a little of the veneer off the truth. He hadn't *really* said he was a reporter.

But the placid Badlam household was suddenly shaken when they received a letter from Sarah Brannan. Edged in black, it told of Tom Brannan's death at eighty-two, observing that: ". . . he found peace towards the last. Drink, which had been his relentless master, was cast off before the end, and he had found serenity by the time he passed on . . ."

It was too late for them to attend the funeral but Sam was hurriedly sent east to comfort his mother, for by now all his brothers had left home and she was completely alone. To Sam's surprise he found that his father, for all his drinking, had left a sizable legacy to his children in addition to providing comfortably for his widow. After a brief visit with his mother, Sam returned to Painesville, where Mary Ann and Alex decided they would invest their inheritance in a store. Typically, Sam announced that he would use his to buy off the remaining year of his apprenticeship.

It didn't take all of his money and for the rest Sam had even grander plans. First, he bought a new wardrobe of high fashion and nothing but the best. At eighteen, he had fulfilled the promise of his youth. He had wavy brown hair, sideburns and a wisp of a goatee, handsome face with brown eyes, and a trim, energetic attitude which spoke vibrant energy.

"Smell the roses, you pass this way but once," Sam replied impudently when his sister chided him about spending so much on clothes.

At loose ends now he had bought his apprenticeship, Sam couldn't wait to spend the rest of his money. With boyish enthusiasm he was looking for quick profits, not long-time investments. He saw the crush of population into Ohio and how townsites were being planned and sold. Why not get in on it?

"You'd better go easy, Sam," Alex counseled. "There's land

sharks a-plenty working this territory, too, and they'll gobble up your money."

"Not if you get in first. That's the ticket to success," Sam argued. "The ones who won't take a chance will pay the price later."

Alex shrugged as he recognized that faraway look on Sam's face. Sam was already jotting up the profits from this venture and pyramiding them into something bigger. "Well, suit yourself but don't whimper when you lose, boy," Alex gave in.

Sam winced at the use of that youthful term, though he knew Alex meant it in affection. "I never have whined, have I? I may get lumps on my head from trying but that's better than calluses on my seat," he replied.

He had reason to reconsider his brash remarks a few weeks later when he lost most of his money, along with thousands of others, in the Ohio land frauds of 1837. "I guess I'm the youngest business failure ever," Sam admitted. "But at least I'm a printer now and no land pirate can take my profession away from me."

"We can give you a job clerking in Alex's store," Mary Ann offered, but Sam refused. Having tangled with the world once, he was anxious to try his luck on his own again. He packed the few things he owned and kissed Mary Ann goodbye. He planned to work his way east, visit their mother, then wander on down to see Tom in New Orleans. He looked vague when Mary Ann asked when he would be back. "I don't really know, sis," he said. "Once you've pulled up the roots of one home you don't settle down again until you've made a new one of your own."

By now Sam's fingers could pick type from a case as fast as a chicken picking corn, and he had little trouble finding jobs. It wasn't long before he had a brief reunion, his last, with his mother. Before he left, she pressed some money in his hand, saying she wanted him to have it, that she had little use for money any longer. The words were prophetic, for she died that December while Sam was in New Orleans.

Through his brother John, who was now first officer aboard a packet, Sam arranged to ship as an ordinary seaman aboard the vessel which was bound for New Orleans. Sam wasn't in any hurry, but by the time they reached their destination he was thoroughly disgusted with the Spartan life, wormy meals and arduous duty of a seaman. But he was never one to be long depressed, especially when he found his brother Tom in New Orleans just at Mardi Gras, the time of carnival which preceded Lent. Both of the Brannan boys, being healthy, vigorous young men, thoroughly enjoyed the revelry, and while they savored a fine bottle of wine in a St. Charles Street inn, they talked of the future.

Tom had some business experience and had saved a little money. Sam pulled his pockets out in a gesture of poverty but enthusiastically boasted that he was the world's best printer. Maybe editor, too. Sam had a persuasive tongue. Together they decided they would start a weekly newspaper. Sam was to gather the news and handle the printing. Tom was to sell advertisements, or cards as they were called, and handle all of the money. The boys shook hands and the plans began.

Once the revelry was over, it was easy to gain the merchants' attentions, especially if one was buying as the Brannans were. They purchased a Washington-Hoe press which needed some repair but seemed worth the price; a few fonts of type, Sam favoring the Cheltenham and Bodoni faces; and some paper stock and set up business in a small, gloomy shop. It wasn't gloomy for long.

After an issue or two had been published, with reasonable success considering their enormous lack of experience, Sam witnessed a slave sale. The sight of human beings being pinched, prodded and probed like animals so revolted him that he wrote an essay which inflamed many of their Southern readers and disenchanted the rest.

"You can threaten me with anything you want," Sam raged
when a man brandished a hickory walking stick at him after
reading his essay. "But I'll never change my opinion about
the vile practice of slavery or the people who indulge in it.
Never."

Tom stood behind Sam, a pinch bar ready for use if any
more irate customers got out of hand. Both Brannans knew
the future of the weekly had been aborted, but they worked
furiously to kindle enough interest to keep the paper alive.

Another issue, the sixth, was locked in its chases on the
composing stones when Tom complained of feeling ill. Sam
closed the shop and took him home. In a matter of hours,
Tom thrashed and burned with a fever. Cool cloths and clear
broth were of no avail against yellow fever. Within two days
Tom was dead, his body collected by one of the dead carts
which roamed the streets during the recurrent plagues in
New Orleans.

Grief-stricken, Sam was glad to leave, and the local residents felt no loss. He stored his press and type, jobbed out
his paper stock and print shop items, and moved northward
without a particular aim, glad only to be quit of the South.

By the time Sam ambled into Indianapolis he had revived
enough to get himself hired as a reporter on the *Gazette*.
Like all reporters of that time, he had the license to write
and print anything he was willing to back up. Sam's interest
in the *Gazette* kindled instantly when he learned the editor
was militantly anti-slavery. But the latter compounded the
mistake that Sam had made. He slashed at his readers with
an editorial broadaxe and offended more than informed. As
a result, pressure was applied and Sam was asked to take over
in the editor's place.

Sam never hesitated for a moment and agreed to try and
save the foundering newspaper. The creditors pressed the
Gazette for money, even though Sam steered a moderate
course in his editorial policies. But the community wasn't
satisfied to let the *Gazette* survive. Machinery, paper stock

and type were seized by the sheriff. Sam sent for his own stored press and type and staved off disaster for a few more issues, but the newspaper had suffered mortal wounds and it expired. At loose ends again, Sam had his press and type crated and shipped on ahead, then boarded a stage for Paines-ville.

Mary Ann and Alex Badlam welcomed him and thought-fully said nothing about his skirmishes with the world. His sister in particular was proud of him and his striking good looks. "Such a handsome boy you are, Sammy," she said as she hugged him.

"Sammy! Boy!" he snorted. "I'm a man now, sis, more'n twenty-one. Show respect for my age and my worldly expe-rience!"

"Sam, you'll never outgrow your boyish enthusiasms," Mary Ann said. "You pick up a penny and imagine it's a dollar. You'll never settle down."

"And why should I?" Sam replied. "I want to travel, have excitement, do new things. That is the way to enjoy life. I started out a printer's devil and I have no ambition to be-come a saint. To get ahead in this life one has to take chances."

Mary Ann shook her head despairingly and exchanged amused glances with her husband. But Sam did not notice. With the rich and booming voice that had come to him with manhood he had already launched into a colorful tale of his past adventures and his even more remarkable plans for the future. There was something about his voice and his enthusi-asm that seemed almost magical, so that for a moment even Mary Ann had the feeling that this big, handsome brother really could make dreams come true.

2 Voyage of the *Brooklyn*

Because Alex and Mary Ann were now vitally involved in the Mormon movement, Sam, as a member of the Badlam household, became involved in church activity, too. He enjoyed the sermons and socials, but not hewing too closely to some of the precepts, he resisted joining at first. He soon changed his mind, however, when he met Harriet Hatch at one of the social functions held in Kirtland. Sam didn't know it but Mary Ann had actually arranged the meeting, hoping that a wife would keep her younger brother in Painesville.

Mary Ann seemed to be right. Sam took to Harriet like a magnet to iron. She was a plain, blonde girl, with a substantial figure and a pleasant disposition. Sam proposed and Harriet accepted. The marriage was officially sealed by Joseph Smith, head of the church, which everyone agreed was an auspicious start. But a start was all that it turned out to be.

Beneath Harriet's plain but pleasant enamel there lurked the hidden disposition of a harpy and Sam was soon made to understand that his place was in the home. Sam's restlessness mounted. When his wife became even more petulant and demanding, his fiery temper exploded. After a particu-

larly bitter quarrel, Harriet declared that she never wanted
to see him again. Sam agreed heatedly and left, telling her
to get a divorce. It would be years before Sam Brannan would
reap the real consequences of this unfortunate, youthful
union. One was his daughter Elmira, born after he left, and
the other was that no divorce was ever secured by Harriet
Hatch Brannan.

Footloose again, Sam accepted a fund-raising assignment in
behalf of the Mormons and went off toward New York. In
the beginning his purpose was more escapist than evangeli-
cal, but his wanderings took on some form when he met William Smith, brother of "The Prophet," Joseph Smith, in New
York. By now Sam had become a convincing orator, able
to easily sway people with his impassioned words. He had
worked hard on the campaign when a brief but severe ill-
ness, which was described as malaria, felled him.

When he resumed his work, he joined Smith, who told
him that a newspaper was being planned in New York, provided funds could be raised. If their solicitation was successful and Sam became an active, tithing member of the church,
Smith promised he would be named editor of the newspaper.
Sam rose to the lure like a trout to a fly and toured the New
England states with his new teammate, his oratory becoming
more impressive with each stop.

After Smith had baptized Sam with the Hudson River
waters he was allowed to share some of the inner church discussions where he learned there was growing dissension between Smith and Brigham Young, one of the leading apostles.
Factions seemed to be forming within the church structure,
but Sam took small interest in these differences, concentrating his concern on the paper. He didn't know Brigham
Young. He did know and like Joseph Smith, so he found
himself designated a Smith adherent and identified with that
group without actual participation.

"The name of the paper will be *The Prophet*," William
Smith told him once they had rented a small office at 7 Spruce

Street in New York City. "It gives a certain dignity to the publication . . ."

"And recalls who is our leader," Sam agreed.

To help splice out the church appropriations for the newspaper, Sam arranged to have his press and type shipped to New York to be used in the publication. Like their owner, they were to travel many thousands of miles before they finally found a permanent home.

The organization of the newspaper called for William Smith to write the editorials, occasionally supplemented by some from his brother Joseph, who was then in Nauvoo, Illinois, having been driven out of Kirtland and Independence, Missouri, along with his people. Two other Mormon officials, Orson and Parley Pratt, contributed poetry and essays while Sam wrote the general news and managed the advertising department.

In addition, Sam had permission to solicit such job work as would supplement the skimpy income which the newspaper was expected to produce. All of the necessary bases seemed to have been touched, and *The, Prophet* quickly became the voice of the Mormons residing in the eastern seaboard area, as Smith had planned.

Sam attacked his job with his customary vigor. He covered the wharves, soliciting printing from the business houses which congregated there; Wall Street, where the financial center of New York seemed to have seeded itself; and political meetings. Sam sought job printing from all hues of the political spectrum, bidding to print their flyers, folders and personal cards.

Sam, who dressed in the flamboyant manner appreciated by those who knew literary men, always introduced himself as the editor of *The Prophet*, the official newspaper of the Latter Day Saints. While Sam never said the actual words, even the thickest-brained ward heeler got the hint that the paper's influence might easily be tipped one way or another, depending upon what work its printing plant received. Sam did not consider himself a liar. He did have influence to cast—his own vote—and in that he was never dictated by church or councilman. He was struggling to keep his paper afloat and he was a man who took chances.

When he had first arrived in New York, William Smith had taken Sam to Widow Fanny Corwin's boardinghouse, a favorite residence for Mormons involved in missionary work.

Mrs. Corwin sat as an overseer and her daughter, who displayed a haughty mantle, did as little as possible waiting on table and had nothing whatever to do with the guests. Perversely, Sam became intrigued with Ann Eliza Corwin. "She's a looker and a real lady," Sam said, completely forgetting his tempestuous affair with Hattie not so long before. At first, Ann Eliza would not permit Sam to talk with her unless her mother was present, but later there were long talks and walks. Sam didn't mention Harriet, because the matter seemed a closed chapter, but he resolved to tell Ann Eliza about it in time, if it were ever necessary.

Since its founding *The Prophet* had done as well as anyone had hoped and Sam had a substantial start on a job printing business on the side. It seemed a propitious time to suggest marriage but then the awesome news came that the thirty-nine-year-old leader Joseph Smith had been murdered by a mob on June 27, 1844, in Carthage, Illinois!

It was the end of the Mormons. Maybe the end of the world!

Trouble had always ridden the long coat-tails of Prophet Joseph Smith, who thought he had finally found a gathering place for his people at Nauvoo after being persecuted and driven from other areas. Nauvoo had become a flourishing center as the movement gained momentum, for it was an attractive, dynamic religion as described by its prophets, apostles, saints and other heavenly messengers. The gatherings offered a helping hand to all; no man was allowed to suffer or despair without being aided by the others. It gained particular strength among newly arrived immigrants because it made an immediate offer of help to the stranger. Though Joseph Smith's original revelations provided for plural marriages, this aspect was seldom discussed by the Mormons in order to avoid further persecution.

The present bloodshed had erupted as a result of a newspaper article which charged Smith and the sect with immorality and misrule. When Smith retaliated and tried to suppress the article, public sentiment was aroused and a mob formed. Smith, his brother Hyrum, John Taylor and Willard Richards were jailed, then spirited off to Carthage to protect them from the mob. But another gang formed and the Smiths were dragged from prison and slain.

With loss of their leader, a power struggle began for leadership of the still new church. Brigham Young had waited in the background too long. When the Smith faction tried to establish a regency for Smith's son, Young moved quickly and his appearance proved timely, crucial and decisive.

Sam Brannan was shaken with the news, but realizing his importance in the cataclysmic events, he wrote carefully of all which had taken place. Because of his identification with Smith, Sam continued to urge continuance of the Smith regency and was temporarily disfellowshipped for this heresy; but various extenuating circumstances were in his favor, particularly his demonstrated energy and organizing ability, and he was soon readmitted. It was to Sam's advantage, for many of his affairs were Mormon-oriented now, and though his marriage to Ann Eliza was solemnized in the Episcopal church, he also insisted that it be "sealed" in Mormon rites as well.

The Pratts, now even stronger in the inner councils, agreed with Sam that the name of the newspaper should be changed to avoid further irritation of the public. *The Messenger* was chosen, and shortly after the change Sam printed a letter from Governor Ford of Illinois. The Governor had set the date of February 1, 1846, as the final day the Mormons would

be permitted to leave Nauvoo peaceably. After that they
would be driven out. In his letter he suggested that they
might find refuge in California because there could be scant
opposition from the Mexicans and Indians there, and a handful of determined men could probably overcome what little
opposition did exist.

Governor Ford had planted a covert suggestion with men
of aggressive ideas. According to Ford, if such a filibuster, or
forceful invasion of a country with which the U.S. was at
peace, was attempted, it must be kept secret, else it would
be incumbent upon the United States to stop it. But he
pointed out that once the Mormons were beyond the U.S.
borders they would be able to act as their consciences allowed.

"Give me a hundred men and we'll take all of California,"
Sam told Brigham Young excitedly. Though they had
mended their differences, the men were still and always would
be two sparking charges when they met. Dreamers and real-
ists have difficulty in adjusting their differences.

"That is not the way, Brother Brannan," Young replied.
He was a stern-faced man, with principles to match. But he
was generous and understanding, a man whom even Sam
described as a titan. Sam had been told he would play an
important part in the exodus of the Mormons which was to
take place soon, for Young had decided that a new Zion
must be found for his people where they could live in peace.
He had petitioned President Polk to provide them with con-
gressional immunity, but his plea had been ignored. It was
apparent that his Saints would have to leave the United
States to seek religious sanctuary farther west.

Young himself planned to lead a contingent overland, out
of Illinois into the wilderness as Moses of old. Sam Brannan
meanwhile was to charter a ship, recruit the Mormons living on the eastern seaboard, and take them around the Horn.
All would meet in California.

For a man who was seldom without something to say, Sam
Brannan for once found himself speechless before the enormity of the task which he had been assigned.

The tocsin was sounded through the columns of *The Messenger* and Sam began to seek an ark. Once circulars were distributed to all of the church members who might be interested, *The Messenger* was suspended, because the printing equipment was a vital part of the plan and had to be packed to go west with them. With the endorsement of Brigham Young, Sam now recruited colonists, chartered a suitable vessel and arranged for freight and clearance.

Captain Richardson, newly a member of the congregation, contacted Sam and suggested they consider his vessel, the *Brooklyn*, which was presently in New York Harbor and available. Sam inspected the five-hundred-ton ship and got an estimate of charter costs, so he could figure expenses. He realized that even at best he would be woefully short. Captain Richardson was asking twelve hundred dollars per month charter fee, plus all port and other charges. The costs of converting the cargo ship into a passenger vessel suitable for carrying more than two hundred people would also have to be borne by the members. Sam was a bit stunned but agreed that the charges seemed fair. He immediately organized "Sam Brannan & Company" as a legal vehicle through which the business affairs could be conducted. Since he was assuming the full responsibility, financial, legal and moral, he also assumed sole authority. This arrangement was completely fair but later led to some confusion as to vested interests.

Sam next went to Washington to press a claim for a mail contract, a bit of revenue which he hoped might help pay expenses. The passenger fares from New York to California had been set at fifty dollars, plus twenty-five for food for each adult; children would go for half-fare.

Zealots of any stripe were not highly regarded in Washington at that time and Sam's initial efforts failed. He finally was shunted off to Amos Kendall, the Postmaster General, who refused the mail contract but suggested a private meeting. Later that day, accompanied by A. G. Benson, owner of a trading company in which Kendall and many other impor-

tant political figures were financially interested, Kendall offered Sam a counter proposal.

"You realize that war with Mexico is almost a certainty
and that Alta California is presently a Mexican province,
don't you?" Kendall asked, after they were seated in Benson's
private office.

Sam felt a surge of excitement as he realized a proposition
was about to be made. It was late 1845 and he did not need
to be told that war with Mexico was becoming more of a
possibility with each passing day, for the Texans who three
years earlier had set up an independent republic were now
talking of annexation to the Union and there was constant
friction along the southern border.

Kendall went on to explain that in event of war California undoubtedly would be one of the first areas seized.
"But while negotiations for a peaceful settlement still continue, our government would hardly look with favor on any
premature move. In fact if it was learned that you Mormons
had such a plan in mind, you would be prevented from sailing." He studied Sam shrewdly.

Sam nodded that he was to continue.

"On the other hand if you announce your intention to sail
to Oregon, which is jointly owned by the United States and
Britain, I am certain we can secure clearance papers for you.
Once you are at sea we can hardly help it if you change your
mind and put into San Francisco Harbor instead."

Sam was no fool; he began to see the plot. "And I suppose
there is a price for this assistance?" he asked.

Kendall nodded. "Mr. Benson's company must be assigned
one half of all the land seized and settled in your first ten
years of occupation."

It was an astounding price and Sam protested. It was one
thing for these officials to skirt a few government regulations
but to seize land for themselves was too much. "That is land
piracy!" Sam exclaimed. "You are little better than thieves.
You are using your position to pressure us because we are

besieged. If we break the law your way, you let us sail. Otherwise you'll righteously have us stopped as filibusters. A very neat robbery."

The faces of the two men reddened with his indictment, but they shrugged. "Take your choice, Mr. Brannan. Those are our terms."

Sam's mind tossed the possibilities back and forth, trying to find a way to overcome the obstacles to each. It was scarcely seconds before a solution presented itself.

"I'm afraid that is a decision which will have to be made on a higher level," Sam said affably. "I have no authority to obligate Brigham Young and the Church of Latter Day Saints to such an arrangement. You draw up the contracts, with a copy for me to sign, and I'll send them along to Young. Meanwhile you can arrange final clearance papers for me from New York to, ah, Oregon."

They all laughed at the joke, but only Sam knew who would be laughing when the final punch line was delivered.

Brannan firmed up his arrangements with Captain Richardson and tentatively set the getaway day as January 12, 1846. Soon the people who had signed the register began straggling into New York, carrying a few belongings. They were quartered with other members in the area until conversion of the ship had been completed.

Sam had liquidated the assets of the newspaper, and the press was brought on board, along with type, paper and necessary supplies. Also loaded on the ship were two portable flour mills, food, cobblers' lasts, sewing machines, hammocks, chickens, cows, pigs, twenty-four stands of arms and ammunition ("to repel pirates"), and a cargo destined for the Sandwich Islands which had been consigned to Sam for one thousand dollars. This shipment was to help defray part of the expenses, which were far from having been met.

Sam felt like the Noah of old as he herded his flock aboard the *Brooklyn*. By now, he had become the father of a son, Sam, Jr., who was carried aboard by Ann Eliza and grand-

mother Fanny Corwin. Many of Sam's other friends and
associates were also in the party, including Ed Kemble and
John Eager, who had been his assistants in the offices of *The
Messenger*. Sam was particularly fond of Kemble, who had
an intellect as dazzling as his own.

The sailing date arrived without anything conclusive having been done about the contract which Kendall and Benson had requested. Sam shrugged away their demands by
pointing out that he had done all he could. If Young hadn't
returned the contract, that was something they would have
to settle with him. Besides, he added significantly, what would
happen if the terms of the contract became known publicly
at this late date? There would be many embarrassed people
who would have difficulty making explanations. The *Brooklyn* had to sail fast. Unless he reached California quickly the
contract could not be fulfilled at all. Kendall and Benson,
having met their match, had to agree.

Meanwhile Brigham Young had organized his own contingent and was already leading his pilgrims overland. Young
would be one prong of an enormous pincer movement; Sam
would be the other. When these two men finally met, an ex-
plosion, which helped shape much of Western history, would
take place.

A brisk wind rattled the rigging of the *Brooklyn* as she put
out to open sea, and the solemn occasion was lightened when
the thin, reedy voice of a child began singing a hymn. One
by one, the other voices slipped into the slow cadence, while
faces bright, scrubbed and hopeful lined the *Brooklyn*'s rails.
Sam Brannan looked at them fondly, then reached into his
pockets and extracted Benson's contract which he had never
bothered to send to Young. The pieces fluttered in the wind,
then were gone. The young man from Saco had successfully
matched wits with two of the shrewdest schemers in Washington.

3 Aloha

When Captain Richardson insisted upon a taut ship, Sam agreed. Aboard the *Brooklyn* there were seventy men, sixty-eight women and one hundred children, two hundred thirty-eight in all. Sam divided them into various "watches" to equally distribute the duties. Even the children were expected to help. Only Ann Eliza refused to take part in the plan, claiming that she was the leader's wife and therefore exempt. Sam refused to make a personal issue of it with her, but there was grumbling among the other passengers.

Sam quieted that quickly. At twenty-seven, he was a commanding figure. He dressed meticulously in clothes which accentuated his muscular six-foot frame. He was endlessly energetic and capable of lightning decisions. While he might be wrong, he seldom was in doubt.

Being the vested authority aboard the vessel required a resolute hand. Accommodations below decks were miserable. Sectioning the area into suitable compartments had left so little space that it was difficult to move about and impossible for adults to stand erect. When the seas became rough, what few furnishings there were hadn't been lashed down and pitched about at will. The pilgrims became ill and there was

scant ventilation anywhere in the cramped quarters. The
stoic resistance to discomfort embraced by most of these people was sorely tested during the voyage. Perhaps it was the
unity fostered by rejection and persecution which gave them
their strength. It was no irony of history that the Mormons,
like the poor and harassed from Europe, were on their way
to build a brave new world.

Resolution they needed, because an albatross of ill fortune followed the ship, it seemed. Ten were to expire during
the long voyage which would take nearly six months.

Sam performed the first funeral service at sea for Ellis En-
sign, who had tottered aboard with his tubercular daughter
Eliza and son Jerusha, hoping to keep their family together
even in their last days. These obviously had not been far
distant when the *Brooklyn* first weighed anchor, for Eliza
soon followed her father in death.

Four children were next to die before the passenger list
finally took a happier turn. A son was born to the Jonathan
Cades. When they couldn't decide upon a name, Sam suggested "Atlantic" in honor of the ocean upon which they
were presently sailing. It was adopted at once, and Sam performed the christening ceremony.

Trouble next appeared aboard ship in a rather unexpected
way when Lucy Eager, a widow, became amorously involved
with two of the elders of the church, Ambrose Moses and
Ward Bell, then later Orrin Smith. All of the men were married and fathers of numerous children. Sam curtly warned
the widow, along with the men, that the flirting and carrying on had to cease forthwith or he would take severe dis-
ciplinary measures. Though all agreed, Sam saw that it was
with a sullen unwilling acceptance of his authority and he
wasn't sure how long it would be respected. There was nothing he could do at the moment but accept their promises.

There had been little relief from the storms during the
first weeks of the trip and soon the *Brooklyn* was fighting
another. She rolled, dipped and plunged, trying to stay afloat

in the raging seas which thundered down the decks. The masts, though barren of sail, waved like wands when Sam was summoned to the Captain.

"She won't make it through this night," Captain Richardson told him. "You'd better prepare your people, both physically and spiritually."

Sam agreed he would break the grim news but suggested that Captain Richardson accompany him. "You don't need to worry about my people," he said proudly. "All will be well."

His estimate proved to be correct. After the announcement of the impending disaster, the pilgrims went quietly about gathering a few items and preparing their children in case they had to abandon ship. There was no panic or fear. Individually each made his adjustment to God, then someone began singing the hymn "The Spirit of God." Soon their spirits lightened and they changed the song to "We're Going to California."

Captain Richardson watched this amazing performance, then returned to his tasks still shaking his head. With such confidence and courage behind him, the Captain found his own determination restored. Even the *Brooklyn* seemed to have found a firmer purchase on the future; for not more than an hour later, the winds stilled as though a heavenly blanket had been thrown over the storm. A heavy ground swell persisted but it quieted too when a bright sun appeared in the sky later that morning. The decks were crowded with the pilgrims kneeling in prayerful thanks for their deliverance.

Though that awesome storm was followed by relative calm while rounding Cape Horn, the fair weather was shattered again off the port of Valparaiso, Chile. They had hoped to put in there to replenish their water supply, which had become so depleted that rationing had to be instituted, but it was impossible to make port.

One woman, Mrs. Laura Goodwin, mother of six children

and the wife of Isaac, was seriously injured in a fall during the violent storm, which drove the *Brooklyn* miles off its course. Realizing that he would have to skirt the storm if he could, Captain Richardson laid a new course for the island of Juan Fernando, which was reached May 4, 1846.

This was Robinson Crusoe's island, the lonely place Defoe had so vividly described in his book. What images it called up for adults and children alike! Over the years the island had alternately flourished and died according to the vagrant political winds which controlled its fortunes.

When the *Brooklyn* anchored off the island it was in one of its decadent spells and only two families lived there. Fortunately for the ship's passengers and crew there was an abundance of wild, tropical fruit and fresh vegetables to diminish the scurvy which had plagued many of them. The water casks were refilled and all drank heavily from the welcome bubbling spring water. Pigs and goats were hunted and killed. A few were eaten and the rest salted down for the remainder of the voyage. Fish were caught and fuel wood was harvested. The stop was a welcome respite for everyone and the intermission took on a holiday air, except for one solemn occurrence.

Mrs. Goodwin finally succumbed to her injuries. Sam read the simple funeral services, and with that task done the passengers and crew filed aboard and the ship got underway again. Now their course was set for the Sandwich Islands to deliver the cargo they were carrying to defray expenses.

Sam had a military organization in training now. Seldom was there a fair day that he didn't yell, "Company formation." Using the fair weather and the clear space of the main deck, he taught his men a manual of arms, along with close-order drill. The latter was largely for discipline rather than any real military significance. Most of his men could use weapons, which was the important part of the operation.

While this was going on, the women chatted and sang as they cut, stitched and hemmed bolts of rough cloth into suitable uniforms for their men. With their display of arms, flourish of drums and trim uniforms, Brannan's Company had the appearance, if not the skills, of a formidable armed band. Though Sam didn't share his thoughts in this matter, he was certain that his seventy determined men could seize all of California if the occasion demanded it. The men seemed to sense his confidence and responded briskly to his commands.

It was June 20, 1846, when they rounded Diamond Head in the Sandwich Islands, now called the Hawaiian Islands. They were one hundred thirty-six days out of New York, excluding the time spent at Juan Fernando, which consumed five days.

Sam peered anxiously at the low-lying islands through his brass-bound telescope and saw there were American warships waiting in the harbor.

"I wonder if the United States and Mexico can be already at war?" Sam asked Ed Kemble, who stood at his side. "Look at the warships at anchor. One is the *Congress*."

Once the *Brooklyn* was tied up to a sagging wooden pier, Sam stepped ashore to arrange for commitment of the cargo. A crowd swarmed to greet them. The Mormons were decked with leis of hibiscus flowers while native boys dived and frolicked in the water. Most of the native women were clothed in Mother Hubbards, indicating that the civilizing process of missionaries had already enlightened these people. Trays of flower-garnished fruits were offered and quickly eaten. Passengers from the ship were whisked away in carriages of all sorts to visit the islands and to stay with residents. It was there too that winsome Mary Addison, not quite twenty, met Henry Harris, son of a wealthy planter, beginning adventures which had far-reaching significance.

After seeing that the cargo was delivered and the money collected, Sam called upon Commodore Robert F. Stockton, ranking officer of the U. S. Navy in the area. He told Sam that his flagship, the *Congress*, was to lead an armed assault on Monterey, California, for war had come between the United States and Mexico on May 12, 1846, while the *Brooklyn* was still at sea.

Stockton also added that Captain Montgomery was somewhere in the Monterey area already, though he wasn't certain of his immediate location.

As they talked Sam remembered his discussions with Kendall and Benson. If the United States seized California first, the Mormons might be no better off than before. Trouble and persecution could follow again. But if they could beat Stockton and the rest of his navy ships to California, they would have a prior claim on the land, a claim which they could demand be honored by the United States. There was no need to maintain the fiction of going to Oregon any longer. He would race to try to take San Francisco Bay before anyone else. It was a daring plan and worthy of Sam's imagination.

It took two weeks to transfer the cargo and get the ship prepared for the final leg of the journey. Strutting about the deck, Sam drilled his men and put them through new martial maneuvers. He could already imagine himself stamping ashore in California at the head of his army.

Sam also approved the application of Henry Harris to accompany them to California, for he and Mary Addison had announced their engagement and planned to be married later. Sam was reluctant about Harris, because it appeared that he might be a cause of trouble and dissent. He vaguely disliked the youth but shrugged away the thought because he knew it had nothing to do with the merit of his application. Besides he had new problems.

When Captain Richardson complained to Sam that the flirting on the part of Widow Eager was again becoming altogether too flagrant, Sam acted quickly. He called the widow, Moses, Smith and Bell before him, advising them that he would prefer charges of misconduct against them and a secular trial would be held.

Sam was the prosecutor; Captain Richardson presided; and young Harris was chosen as defense attorney. The accused four were found to be guilty of misconduct and expelled from the church. The decision was severe and caused a good deal of dissension among members of the passenger list.

Thus it was with a new and unwanted feeling of tension that the *Brooklyn* finally sailed for California on July 1, 1846, even the lingering "alohas" failing to clear the troubled way ahead.

4   That Flag Again!

With her sails fully leafed out, the *Brooklyn* pushed great hoops of cottony fog ahead of her as she slipped past the rocky cluster called the Farallon Islands, a few miles from the Golden Gate, the entrance to San Francisco Bay.

"I swear you've spent most of your time since we left the Sandwich Islands on the quarter-deck, Sam," Ed Kemble observed. "Don't you ever get tired of watching?"

Sam answered him by closing his eyes to slits in an effort to peer ahead. It was July 31, 1846, when the bowsprit of the vessel finally punctured the fog of the Golden Gate and the gray curtain dropped behind them as they slid into calm waters in the warm sunshine.

Sam clenched his hands excitedly as he got his first view of the Bay and the Mexican village of Yerba Buena. A few ships rode at anchor, beyond was a scattering of shacks and here and there some adobe and timber buildings. He aimed his long, brass-bound telescope inland. The glass roved and circled, then riveted on one target. Sam's smile slipped away; his face tightened into a scowl. He lowered the telescope, grabbed off his flat-brimmed beaver hat and slammed it to the deck.

"Damn it, there's the flag!" Sam thundered. "They beat us!"

Ed Kemble grabbed the glass. Flying above one of the adobe buildings was the Stars and Stripes. U. S. forces had beat them to the conquest. "You should have been first, Sam," he agreed sadly. "You should have been first to raise the flag."

Sam was silent, then he shrugged away his disappointment and his smile returned. "Yes, it's too bad, Ed. But the only people who don't have disappointments are those who never take a chance."

"No one will ever accuse you of that!" Ed said.

Like Sam, the other members of his company were disappointed because they had hoped to establish their colony independent of the United States, where they had suffered so much persecution. But while all might not be as resilient as Sam, they were of the stuff which made great pioneers. Yelling back that he would have all of the details soon, Sam skittered down the Jacob's ladder into a newly arrived naval launch which rocked at its foot. A short time later he was being piped aboard the *U.S.S. Portsmouth* and warmly welcomed by Captain John B. Montgomery, the ship's master.

"Welcome aboard! Welcome to the newest possession of the United States—Alta California," the handsome officer said. "You are our first visitors. Are you planning to stay?"

"Yes, I am here to stay," Sam replied as he shook hands with Montgomery. "I believe the rest will remain and others are coming overland to join us."

Though the *Brooklyn* clearance papers weren't entirely in order since they indicated Oregon as their destination, Montgomery was not about to fuss over petty details. He issued orders to his first officer to assist in landing the Mormons and to help them take possession of whatever shacks they could find available.

"We are people of peace," Sam said, "and we come with

good will. I want to declare a few stand of arms we have and put them at your disposition."

Montgomery's face flashed surprise but he said they could be stored until arrangements had been made. Sam also suggested that his people rip off the insignia to convert their uniforms into work clothes.

Sam, the Brannan family, Captain Richardson, and several others were quartered in Casa Grande, the out-sized adobe building which was on Washington and Montgomery Streets.

In many ways, Sam seemed to have stepped on the starter button of California history when he landed at Yerba Buena. But he had at least one enemy. No sooner was she ashore than Widow Lucy Eager filed charges against Sam with Captain Montgomery, alleging all sorts of high and low crimes. Montgomery discussed the matter with Sam, then dismissed the complaint. "Even if I thought Mrs. Eager was right, there is nothing I'd do. It is a secular matter, of interest only to Mormons," he ruled. Unfortunately not everyone in the company agreed.

Sam's quick wit and geniality were a welcome addition to the town and Sam responded warmly to the friendship offered him. Washington Bartlett, detached from the *Portsmouth* to replace the Mexican alcalde, resented Sam's popularity. As they shared some drinks at the Casa Grande bar, Bartlett suggested Sam be given the Royal California welcome, winking knowingly at the others.

"That sounds good to me," Sam said. "What do I do?"

Bartlett directed Sam toward the door for the initiation ceremonies, with the other men following, eager to witness the fun.

"We blindfold you, whirl you about, then you try to reach the flagpole on the far side of the Plaza before we count one hundred," Bartlett explained the rites.

Sam nodded and was blindfolded. After being whirled around he was aimed in the general direction of the flagpole. The count began: "one, two, three . . ." His arms outstretched like a sleepwalker's, Sam walked slowly toward the pole, which happened to be surrounded by a mudhole several inches deep in water. Because the soil was adobe clay, it was extremely slippery when wet.

"Go, Sam, go," the crowd chanted. They continued the count, ". . . forty-six, forty-seven . . ."

Sam wandered off course, but as his hands touched onlookers they guided him back toward the target. Finally he stepped into the mud trap. His feet slipped from under him and his hands clawed at the air. With a splash and skid he landed on his back in the slimy mudhole. But Sam made no move to tear off the blindfold and disqualify himself. The crowd watched for a moment in silence, then someone yelled helpfully:

"No, Sam, a little to your right, then straight on." Others yelled encouragement now, giving him directions as he slipped, fell, recovered himself and kept going. The count, being called now only by Bartlett, had barely reached seventy-three when Sam finally felt the pole and hauled himself erect. Once on his feet, he whipped away the blindfold. Though his fine clothes were bedraggled and dripping, his teeth blazed in a smile through his mud-blackened face.

"I win. I'm a member now," Sam yelled. "Since I have successfully passed the test of royalty I must have a rank. Let's see. How about . . . Caliph of California?"

There was a thunderous roar of approval which grew even louder when Sam yelled that he would stand for drinks for everyone. Later, he proposed a toast to Bartlett: "To you, Washington Bartlett, for making me 'Caliph of California,' because while the mud will wash off my clothes, these friends and memories will last forever."

Bartlett was equal to the situation. "I must confess, Sam, you conquered California today even more effectively than the men of the *Portsmouth*." The two men shook hands.

The village of Yerba Buena, Spanish for "good herb," which one day would become the city of San Francisco, con-

sisted at that time of nine adobe buildings and a scattering
of spit and paper shacks. The population was made up of a
few Mexican families, fewer than a dozen resident Americans,
about one hundred Indians and the seventy-odd men of the
U.S.S. Portsmouth. Brannan's new arrivals more than out-
numbered the entire population and his semi-trained volunteers made a welcome addition to the military garrison and
were quickly organized into a home guard.

While he counseled and aided his people in getting settled,
Sam was pressed with an even more immediate problem. He
was still short $1,000 on the transportation charges owed
Captain Richardson. Since he had assumed the responsibility,
the captain was looking to him for payment. Fortunately,
Sam was a man of ideas. Cash was out of the question, but
learning that unlimited redwood could be logged in the for-
ests across the bay, he persuaded the captain to accept his payment in a cargo of prime redwood.

When only a few men volunteered to help fell the trees,
Sam exercised his rank and ordered the necessary hands to
the job, providing them with whipsaws, axes and *caretas*
drawn by boney Spanish oxen. The *Brooklyn's* deck soon
was piled with huge logs, and its satisfied captain sailed out
of San Francisco, leaving the colonists to continue their work
of making a new home.

Even with tottering finances, Sam arranged credit for food
and supplies to be used by members of the Company. He saw
that religious needs were met, too, by preaching the first non-
Catholic sermon given in California and performing the first
non-Catholic marriage ceremony when Lizzie Winner and
Basil Hall were "sealed" in Mormon rites. Washington Bartlett winced with displeasure at being eclipsed by Sam's activities.

But it appeared that Bartlett might triumph when he was
called on to preside over the first court session convened under the American aegis. It was not surprising that Sam, rapidly proving himself as first in so many other things, should

appear in this court session also as the first defendant. He was charged with misuse of community funds by Henry Harris, whom he had taken aboard in the Sandwich Islands. Harris had represented Widow Eager and other dissidents at the disfellowship proceedings and apparently some of their dissatisfaction had rubbed off on the newcomer.

"You are charged, Samuel Brannan, with misuse of funds," Bartlett read.

Sam entered an innocent plea and added he didn't believe the case was a criminal one. "At best it is a civil or even an ecclesiastical matter," Sam said, "but out of deference to the court's jurisdiction and in the belief that these scurrilous charges should be laid to rest, I will submit to trial only to provide the forum for a public airing."

Sam marshaled his defenses, hoping an acquittal would preclude future challenges to his authority and that time should then heal the schisms.

Harris had filed the charges because he and his bride wished to leave the area and needed funds. He claimed an interest in the Sam Brannan Company, but Sam scoffed at the charges.

"Dignity of an answer shouldn't be accorded such claims," he said as he paced slowly before Alcalde Bartlett's bench. "Spite prompts this action because Mr. Harris was unsuccessful in his defense of Widow Eager. Moreover, since the Sam Brannan Company was organized in New York, Harris has no claim or contact on which to base such charges."

Sam paused. "Mr. Harris is entitled to take whatever he brought aboard the *Brooklyn* at the Sandwich Islands. Nothing more. However, if he wishes to press his claims and they are sustained, I will advise that the Sam Brannan Company arrived in San Francisco in debt by one thousand dollars. I am quite willing to allow him to share in that if he wishes."

Bartlett smiled at Sam's logic and promptly dismissed the charges, amid cheering and applause, but Sam saw some scowls, too.

In preparation for the gathering with the others whom Young was leading overland, the pilgrims busily set about building homes, businesses and demonstrating their usual industry. Soon the flour mills were operable and the bakers were busy. Others set up workshops as carpenters, cobblers and saddle makers. Meanwhile, Sam launched the business he knew best: a newspaper and printing plant. There was job printing of all sorts, especially from Bartlett and other military officials. With Ed Kemble and John Eager as his assistants, Sam erected his press, distributed type and opened his print shop and newspaper plant near the intersection of Clay and Kearney streets.

"Gonna call this one 'The Messenger'?" Kemble asked.

"Nope," Sam replied with finality. "This paper is to be a new star in the west . . . 'The California Star.'"

" 'Shooting Star' might be more appropriate, Sam," Kemble teased.

Sam joined in the laughter, then quickly sobered. "I have written a small statement of policy which I think will set most folks straight and show that we mean to print the news as it happens." He unfolded a small piece of paper and read: "It shall be our purpose to invoke and defend the rights of all the people against oppression, diffuse accurate information, detect and expose tyranny and *eschew all sectarian issues.*"

Much of the preliminary work on *The Star* was left to Kemble and Eager because Sam was busy discussing with Ezekial Merritt, a gamey old mountain man, the best site for a second Mormon colony. Merritt suggested an area at the confluence of the San Joaquin and Stanislaus rivers which enclosed thousands of well-watered fertile acres and abounded with game of all sorts. Enthusiastically, Sam bought a small launch, the *Comet,* and began plans for the colony, which he called "New Hope."

Sam chose Bill Stout to head a contingent of twenty other colonists, who all seemed delighted with the site. The *Comet* was heavily laden with tools and supplies, and they purchased oxen and stock from a Yankee settler named Robert

Livermore. Stout's men quickly constructed a log house, ploughed and seeded the land and enclosed the entire area with a branch and thatch fence.

Sam was building his own home at Washington and Stockton streets, which would ultimately become the social and cultural center with Ann Eliza Brannan presiding. It was more than Sam could really afford and he stretched his credit as a concession to his wife because of her peevishness with his attention to business rather than family affairs. "She thinks I should be there for teas and such things," Sam told Kemble. "But those things cost money. I told her she's got to make a choice: money or me."

E. P. Jones, a Kentucky lawyer and owner of the Portsmouth House, became editor of *The Star* when Kemble enlisted in the U. S. forces of John C. Fremont still fighting in Southern California. Jones, a green-spectacled, bilious-looking man, was fluent in Spanish and a long-time Yerba Buena resident. Sam, Jones and Eager put together a sample issue of the newspaper called *"Extra Advance of The Star,"* on October 24, 1846. Production problems were solved with this early edition, issued in four pages of 13 x 18-inch size. Eager justified the type, locked up the forms and placed them on the bed of the Washington press. The ink was applied with a brayer, Sam spun the wheel and the threaded shaft lowered the press plate and squeezed the sheet of newsprint. With delight Sam yanked off his first impression, dated January 9, 1847. "There she is. The first *Star* in the West," he shouted.

The Star, even at a thumping six dollars per year, was an immediate success. The job printing business proved equally profitable. Sam seemed to have the affinity for success largely because he applied the energy to create the winning climate.

But *The Star* had competition from *The Californian,* published by Robert Semple at Monterey, the seat of the Mexican colonial government prior to the arrival of the Americans and still the capital for occupation forces.

"The Californian's offer to exchange papers," Sam wrote, "is a barefaced attempt to swindle us." He further noted that

the publishers were lying sycophants and lickspittles, but he finally agreed *The Star* would be sent to them to serve as a model of journalistic elegance and superiority.

Sam thrived on the press of business and personal problems, just as he delighted in the warm fellowship he found at the long polished bar of the Portsmouth House, drinking with the local dignitaries: Montgomery, Colonel Mason, Liliburn Boggs, Kanaka Davis and others. Everyone knew Sam, most people liked him immediately and Sam thrived on that, too.

He was disturbed with reports of growing dissension at the New Hope colony. Stout, according to Sam's informant, had seized certain advantages, and with the resentments engendered the whole project was sinking into a morass of bitterness and self-seeking. Sam planned a visit soon, but first another, far more important task demanded his attention.

In the second issue of *The Star*, January 16, 1847, a story appeared on page two:

EMIGRANTS IN THE MOUNTAINS

"It is probably not generally known to the people that there is now in the California mountains, in a most distressing situation, a party of emigrants from the United States, who were prevented from crossing the mountains by an early, heavy fall of snow. . . ."

In other issues and in his well-known oratory, Sam issued continued pleas and appeals, ultimately resulting in a mass meeting during which $1500 was raised to help these stranded emigrants, an enormous sacrifice for the few residents. On February 13, 1847, Sam Brannan's efforts bore fruit when a twenty-man rescue party, heavily laden with supplies and provisions, headed for the emigrants' camp in the Sierra Nevadas. The stranded wagon train for which Sam had mobilized money, men and materials was the well-known and tragic Donner Party.

5 The Titans Meet

The fighting in California during the Mexican War was of
short duration. When Brannan and his colonists arrived, the
northern section of the colony was already in American hands
and by January 13, 1847, Fremont's forces in the south had
brought the remaining Californianos to accept the mutually
agreeable terms of the Treaty of Cahuenga. However, there
was no way in which such a quick and successful conclusion
could have been anticipated in the East, and as Sam watched
Colonel Jonathan Stevenson's New York Volunteers debark
from the *Thomas H. Perkins*, he felt a twinge of apprehen-
sion. A special contingent, many of whom had been recruited
from the tough Bowery section of New York, they had arrived too late for the actual fighting but would undoubtedly
remain as occupation forces. "They look like trouble," Sam
observed as he stood with two friends watching the men el-
bow their way ashore.

A few days later at the Casa Grande bar when the Colonel
introduced Sam to his officers, including a glowering, bearded
lieutenant named Sam Roberts, there was little reason to
change this opinion. Roberts surveyed Sam Brannan coolly,
then turned away with a sneer. "Turkey-necked Bible-

beater". . . . Sam caught part of Roberts' muttered observa-
tion to another soldier.

Sam had immense pride in his village, yet even before the
arrival of the added population of the New York contingent,
the little settlement was taking on a worldly aspect with its
450 residents. Aware of this shifting of activity from Monterey, the former Mexican capital, Semple had moved his newspaper *The Californian* north to actively compete with Sam's
Star, but there was business enough for both. And temporarily Sam and Washington Bartlett forgot their differences long
enough to take an important step in promoting the future of
the village.

General Vallejo, a leading figure among the Californianos,
Tom Larkin, the newly-appointed American consul at Monterey, and Robert Semple had decided that a new community
on the other side of the Bay should be the future metropolis
and planned to name it Francisca, in honor of the general's
wife, Doña Maria Francisca Felipe Benicia Carillo Vallejo.
Because the name of San Francisco Bay was already widely
known, Bartlett and Sam realized that the repetition of the
name in the new development would divert trade away from
Yerba Buena. Bartlett issued a proclamation which renamed
Yerba Buena as San Francisco. Semple realized the shrewd
gambit had scuttled his plan and changed the name of his
town to Benicia, another of Mrs. Vallejo's names.

Sam trained his editorial guns on Bartlett shortly after the
naming of San Francisco when he uncovered evidence that
the alcalde was using his position to commandeer stock and
other supplies as a "war measure." Sam had gotten on to the
story when his shop had printed some "notes of hand" re-
deemable by the government. When Bartlett was evasive
about the terms of these, Sam's curiosity was piqued. Further
investigation revealed that Bartlett was also seizing lands
and granting deeds for certain considerations.

With proof in hand, Sam reported the matter to Captain

Montgomery, who immediately relieved Bartlett from duty, replacing him with George Hyde, then Edwin Bryant.

Sam had been detained in San Francisco longer than expected because of these and other business affairs. The time had come for his rendezvous with Brigham Young to lead the Mormons into California for the great "gathering."

Sam rode out of San Francisco on April 4, 1847, accompanied by Charley Smith, who would take care of the fifteen-horse train. Their first objective was the headquarters of the wilderness empire carved out by Captain John Sutter, a Swiss emigrant who several years earlier had secured a large land grant from the Mexican government.

Sutter's fort, which stood near the confluence of the Sacramento and American rivers, was a massive adobe bastion. The twelve-foot walls formed a palisade to enclose an entire city, replete to cannon and a small army of Kanakas, who drilled smartly in their hunter-green uniforms and wide-brimmed hats. It was also the supply point and destination of most of the emigrant trains coming over the mountains.

"Welcome, welcome," Captain Sutter greeted them at the end of their upriver trip. Sutter, forty-four, goateed, rotund and merry-eyed, resembled a wilderness Santa Claus and was in sharp contrast with the dark, gaunt, taciturn man standing beside him, whose name was Jim Marshall.

Despite Sam's protests that he was in a hurry, Sutter insisted they stay over and rest. While they ate, Sutter expansively described how his fort hummed with industry and his fields were thick with stock of every sort. Sutter also related some of the horrors of the Donner Party and noted that some of the survivors were still living there with him, following rescue by his supply trains and the welcome addition of the supplies sent from San Francisco.

"We'll have no trouble getting over the mountains, Captain," Sam said. "This early snow is frozen and we'll ride the crust."

But Sutter insisted that Sam inspect the entire fort before leaving. He even suggested that Sam open a store within the enclosure. There was ample space, and though there was little hard money, he pointed out that the trade was always brisk in hides and tallow.

Sam realized that with the California population rapidly increasing such a store should prosper, but for now he had more pressing matters.

Sam and Smith pushed on over the Sierras, through what is now known as Donner Pass. Along the way, they met one tragic straggler from the disaster, Lewis Keseberg, the pariah accused by the others of cannibalism. Crippled with a broken leg, he had been left to die. Sam Brannan reined up and talked with him briefly, then gave him some food and a fresh mount. When Smith objected Sam replied:

"I don't care what the man has done," he said. "I can't sit in final judgment of him. Maybe we don't share his guilt but we share his responsibilities."

Probably because of Sam's aid, Keseberg survived to later play a strange part in Brannan's own life.

Sam pushed on rapidly, passing the grim site of the Donner tragedy and dropping down the eastern slope of the mountains into what seemed an even greater wilderness. It was June before they learned for certain that they could find Young at the Green River encampment in Wyoming, the site chosen for the annual meeting and trading of furs for supplies by the trappers working in the Rocky Mountains. Despite the long days in the saddle, Sam, who was as urban as a city sidewalk, had enjoyed this new experience and temporary freedom from business and social demands. Along the long trail he also had found time to consider his forthcoming discussions with Young. He had to persuade Young to come all the way to California with their people; he could conceive of no other alternative.

Remnants of the midday meal were just being cleared away

when Sam and Smith finally rode into the Brigham Young encampment on June thirtieth. The Green River flowed briskly on the far side of the cottonwood trees.

"Welcome, Brother Brannan," Young said in a pleasant but not overly warm tone. Young was simply dressed in a rough frock coat buttoned to the chin, his craggy, bearded face topped by a round-crowned, wide-brimmed hat. Yet, for all his simple dress, he managed to convey an impression of great strength, and his piercing gray eyes were those of a dedicated visionary.

Sam replied in a manner so casual that it might have appeared these men had parted minutes instead of months before and thousands of miles away. When Sam had dismounted, they began discussions without further preliminaries.

Enthusiastically, Sam sketched the wonders of California, but Young remained passive and unimpressed. Sam learned that in addition to the families journeying west, five hundred of the younger men had joined the Mormon Battalion, organized like Stevenson's Volunteers to fight in the Mexican War, and would rejoin the others when they were no longer needed along the border or in California. He also learned that Young had changed his mind about coming to California.

In Sam Brannan, California had its first booster, but the more persuasive he made his argument, the less interested Young appeared to be.

"It seems to me that you speak more from the heart than the head," Young rumbled. "I realize that the Great Basin area near Salt Lake may not compare with California but it has been recommended to me by our scouts. And there is something else to consider, Brother Brannan. California will now become a part of the United States and we may well be persecuted as before. Don't forget these are the same people who murdered the Prophet and drove us into the wilderness. If we choose a place which is remote and must be wrested from nature, then it is less likely that anyone will covet our Zion or disturb us," Young continued with inexorable logic.

"Yes, but even when you develop the area, you still won't have much," Sam argued. He knew that Young was not only determined but entirely equal to the task which he set for himself and his people. "In California, there's hardly any winter and you have access to sea ports."

"In our kingdom of hope, there'll be no winter," Young said simply. "And we will be self-sufficient."

Sam sensed the finality of his words and the futility of further argument. He rose abruptly and strode from the tent without another word or gesture. Young made no move to call him back.

Next day, they met again but only for Sam to explain about the finances and obligations of his Company and how income had fallen far short of expenses. What tithes he had collected—the Lord's fraction required of all Saints—were necessary to liquidate obligations and bolster credit in getting established in California. They discussed the matter at some length and Young appeared satisfied, since he made no further effort to explore the subject.

Both Young and Sam hesitated to resume discussion as to the final location of the Mormons because they realized their aims were poles apart. Fortunately, Sergeant Williams, a scout from one segment of the Mormon Battalion, rode in. No longer needed to fight in California, they had been seeking out Young and it was only by chance they had wandered as far north as the Green River gathering.

Young asked Sam Brannan if he would return with Williams to guide the rest of the Battalion back so they could join the rest of Young's pilgrims. Sam immediately accepted, thinking that some of the Mormons might be persuaded to go to California rather than Salt Lake, after he had talked with them.

It was near the end of July before Sam and the sergeant

caught up with the Battalion and led them toward the valley of the Great Salt Lake.

"That may be the 'Promised Land' to Young," Sam observed sarcastically when he first saw the Salt Lake area, "but it looks more like the Poisoned Land to me."

The soldier riding beside him agreed that it was bleak and uninviting, but added that Young was a sound thinker and his choice might, in the long run, prove to be best.

"But I've lived in California," Sam said, "and I know what I am talking about. Young just thinks he knows."

"Faith is a great thing even on barren ground," the soldier said, and Sam had to agree.

But he never concealed his disapproval of Young's decision, even though Sam saw the sage-littered area was already being reclaimed and ploughed for crops. With the choice made, Sam was anxious only to get back to California. He did not wear defeat well and he knew there would be a new baby waiting by the time he returned to San Francisco. He rolled that name, San Francisco, about in his mouth. How sweet it seemed, especially after this disappointing trip.

The Mormons were entitled to mustering-out pay, but their captain didn't have enough cash available and a trip to the paymaster in San Francisco would be necessary. Young asked Sam and Charley Smith if they would guide Captain Brown and a companion, Squires, to California; another Mormon would also accompany them as far as Fort Hall to secure supplies.

Sam agreed but immediately regretted his decision when Young entrusted the captain with certain confidential church papers addressed to Mormons on the coast. Sam seethed with the affront, especially since there had been no announced change in the church hierarchy, of which Sam was a member. Silently, he decided that he owed no further allegiance to either Young or the church. Sam made his displeasure apparent when he rode away on August 9, 1847 with the remark that he was glad to be quit of "this place . . ."

His disposition didn't improve as they continued toward California. Finally his disappointment and frustration boiled over. "You may be some great shakes in the Army," he snapped when the Captain objected to the fast pace at which they were riding, "but your rank doesn't impress me. If you want to do things my way, fine. Otherwise shift for yourself."

Sam gouged his heels into his roan's flank and waved Charley Smith to speed up. They rapidly drew away from the others, gradually increasing their lead to a day's ride. Brown and Squires had to track Sam and Smith to follow the trail, as they were no longer in sight.

It was late afternoon on September 8th when they reached Sutter's Fort again, and the smiling Captain Sutter welcomed them back. "What success? When will your Mormons arrive?" he called.

"They won't be here!" Sam said bitterly. "Brigham Young will locate in the Great Basin country near Salt Lake. But I am back to stay and I might be interested in opening that store after all," he added.

Sam, Smith and Sutter discussed business prospects as they consumed a huge dinner of game and trout, topped with Sutter's own brandy. The Captain's enthusiasm touched Sam's own well springs of ebullience, and he forgot the disappointment of the past weeks.

In November Sam returned to Sutter's Fort where, with Sutter's approval, he and Smith opened their new store.

Because Sam would have too many other demands on his time, the store was to be called "C.C. Smith & Company," and Charley Smith would remain at the Fort and operate the new enterprise. Sam's contribution would be to handle the San Francisco sales, including the ordering and reshipment of goods up and down the broad Sacramento River. Despite its formal name, once the store was opened and customers learned that Sam was connected with it, they dubbed it more familiarly: "Brannan's Shirt-tail Store."

The honor of placing the first order went to Captain Sutter, who purchased a list of supplies to be sent to Jim Marshall, who was presently building a sawmill on the American River near a place which the residents called Coloma, after the Cullumah Indians who lived there.

Despite the abrupt change of course his career had made following the talks with Brigham Young, Sam adjusted quickly to the new situation and his own conscience. Before he returned to San Francisco he visited the New Hope colony and, because of the conditions he found there, decided that it was to be dissolved, at least as far as his guardianship was concerned.

Curiously, the source of dissension, William Stout, was now the one who clung to the colony, insisting that it be continued. Stout stubbornly refused to relinquish possession of the house in which he lived and the lands around it and had to be forcibly dispossessed when Sam announced that the lands and other materials were to be auctioned off so all the participants would share in the proceeds after all outstanding obligations had been paid.

There was a good deal of grumbling from Stout and some of the others, but Sam ignored them. He had been in charge when the colony was organized and he still had control. If any of them wanted to remain, all they had to do was to bid on the property when it was put on the block. With that, Sam continued on to San Francisco.

As he rode, he planned for the future. With some rancor he recalled the high hopes and enthusiasm he had carried with him to the meeting with Young. Sam snorted when he thought of anyone choosing Salt Lake over San Francisco Bay. His next move must be the dissolution of Sam Brannan & Company, the legal vehicle he had created to accommodate community affairs after they left New York. That would cut away the final ties, and he felt better having made his decision and charted a new course.

He always did.

6 The Pied Piper

"Sam, I'm glad you're back," Elbert Jones, active editor of *The Star,* said as Sam stopped by his newspaper office even before going home to see his family. "Sam Roberts, Stevenson's lieutenant, has started a racist group which calls themselves 'The Supreme Order of the Star-Spangled Banner.' They've been causing all sorts of trouble with the foreigners here, especially the Chilenos." Jones' face mirrored real concern as he told Sam that the Roberts group, made up of soldiers with too much idle time, was organized along racial and religious lines, including all of the mummery of secret passwords and handshakes. Sam vaguely knew of the movement, for he once had been offered a membership, which he had indignantly refused. He had dismissed the matter from his mind at the time. Now he realized that he should have been more concerned.

"My family all right? How about the baby?" Sam asked the more pressing question. Jones assured him everyone was fine and in addition to his son, he now had a baby daughter, Adelaide. "But this Roberts and his toughs. This won't be any place to raise a family, Sam, if something isn't done," Jones persisted.

"Isn't it typical that a bunch of roughs should wrap their club in such a patriotic name," Sam observed. "And I suppose they're indignant when anyone questions their motives. You say they claim they are doing this to keep California for the Californians—the *white* Californians? Don't suppose they even remember that we stole it from the Mexicans ourselves."

Jones nodded and said that Roberts' bunch met at the deadfall called "The Shades," which was always draped with patriotic bunting and slogans.

Sam decided to talk with Colonel Stevenson and asked him to keep his troops, including officers, out at their encampment at the Presidio, especially during the upcoming elections. Knowing that Jones was a candidate for a city council seat, he had more than a casual interest in seeing that the polling was orderly.

Sam's request was heartily endorsed by Colonel Stevenson, and later, after Jones had won the election, Roberts openly threatened Sam because of his interference.

"Roberts, in a battle of wits you are only half armed, so don't overmatch yourself," Sam quipped, and Roberts was furious. He would have thrashed Sam except that Brannan was too popular and well known for him to take such an overt action, but he warned that the contest wasn't over.

Ed Kemble next took over as editor of *The Star* when Jones entered politics, for Sam became heavily involved in his store at Sutter's Fort. But with San Francisco growing, along with his own family, Sam found time to take the lead in sponsoring a school for youngsters of the area. When the City Council pleaded poverty, Sam dug in his pockets and came up with $100 in gold. He threw it on the table. "There . . . if you're so danged poor, that'll give you a start!" he cried. He had sufficiently shamed the others so that before he left there was $600 heaped on the table, and $1000 by that week's end, assuring San Francisco its first school, which was later erected on Portsmouth Square.

Bill Howard and Henry Mellus, two young San Francisco merchants who were as enthusiastic about California's future as Sam, agreed to provide him with unlimited credit to obtain supplies for his "shirt-tail store." And Sutter's launch, *Dice Mi Nada,* was often nearly awash with its load of supplies on its trips up the Sacramento River to Sutter's Fort.

Sam advertised dissolution of both the Sam Brannan Company and the New Hope colony by inserting notices of merchandise being available. The offer was explicit right down to wicking, twine and castor oil. Returns were divided among those still having an interest in the projects, and the remainder which went unsold was probably later disposed of by Sam because no one else took the initiative or made the effort to do so themselves. Sam was no more averse to a profit than anyone else.

"I should have been a native Californian," Sam told Ed Kemble as he outlined his plans for a special booster edition of *The Star* for attracting residents to California. Sam's special edition was another first of its kind, and such booster papers are still issued in California and elsewhere. "This'll bring hundreds, maybe thousands of people out here," Sam predicted with his usual self-confidence.

"Thousands?" Ed queried. "How in the world would they all get here? Where would they all stay? Sam, you've always got your eye in the sky."

"I am twenty-nine years of age," Sam snapped, "and I didn't come out here to listen to opportunity knock on someone else's door. I'll be able to hear it because I'll be listening."

Dr. Victor J. Fouregard, a San Francisco physician, was hired to assemble the edition of 2,000 copies which was to be distributed in the eastern section of the United States. Sam arranged for dispatch riders, similar to those who would carry the overland mail much later, to carry the papers, along with some special mail which he hoped would pay costs for the entire project. Sam seldom overlooked an opportunity for profit, but the booster edition, like most other Brannan-sponsored projects, was for the general welfare as well as his own.

With the project's aims sketched in, Sam, along with Fouregard, Kemble, Eager and even ex-editor Jones, began writing and setting type for the big edition. California and all of its resources were in the process of being described in heroic prose when Sam had to pay a visit upriver to Sutter's Fort. The area surrounding the Fort was now becoming known as Sacramento, after the large river which drained most of northern California and skirted the west side of the growing settlement.

In the store, Sam and his partner Charley Smith were discussing the inventory, which bulged with everything from treacle to tea and from spice to Dutch schnapps, when a roughly dressed bearded man strode in.

"Gimme some flour, bacon and a jug o' brandy," he ordered. Sam filled the order, placed the goods on the counter, then totaled the bill. "What do you have to trade?" Sam asked.

The man felt in his ragged coat pocket, then came up with a doeskin pouch. He grabbed Sam's hand and held it palm up as he carefully poured some of the sack's contents on the hand: gold dust and small nuggets!

Sam's mouth dropped open, then he exploded: "Gold! Where did that come from?" Sam controlled his excitement. There had been other gold strikes in California, such as the one down in Placerita Canyon in southern California a few years before. That hadn't amounted to anything. "Where did you get it?" Sam persisted, nevertheless.

"Up on the American River where Sutter is having a sawmill built," the man, who was named Jake Wittmer, said. "It was on January 24th, I think. Found a little in the tail race, but there's lots more of it around! Don't say nothing, though. It is a good thing and we'll keep it here for us."

While Sam Brannan was certain that the material was gold, and Wittmer said others had already confirmed it, he left the store to talk with Captain Sutter. Sutter reluctantly admitted that he knew of a small strike but had kept the find secret because the title to his vast land holdings hadn't been confirmed. Sutter also admitted that gold *per se* didn't interest him much because his real dream was to create a wilderness empire built on the real substance of land, agriculture and allied industry.

"All right, maybe I am being selfish," Sutter admitted, pacing the floor of his private office. "But there have been gold strikes before and they never amounted to anything. As yet we have no proof this one will last either. At least I want to make sure I have a clear title to my farmlands before a lot of madmen come tramping up here, ruining my fields."

"I wouldn't say you were being selfish, just wise," Sam replied. Momentarily, some of his own enthusiasm had faded, and lacking anywhere better to keep the gold dust, he put it in the bottom of a small, empty quinine bottle. Viewed a second time, it did not look like quite so much.

But others were learning of the gold found in the tail race at Marshall's new sawmill and in the river nearby. Sam liked to be first in everything, and it hurt when his rival *The Californian* scooped him with the first story about the discovery in its issue of March 15, 1848.

GOLD MINE FOUND

In the newly made raceway of the Saw Mill recently erected by Captain Sutter, on the American River, gold has been found in considerable quantity. . . . California is rich in mineral wealth . . . great chances here for scientific capitalists. Gold has been found in almost every part of the country. . . .

However, his pride was somewhat assuaged by the fact that the rival editors apparently did not consider the news of great importance, for the story appeared on an inside page where it was completely overshadowed by news of a local horserace.

But Sam felt impelled to offer some kind of reply. On May 29, 1848, he published a notice in *The Star:* "ALL SHAM: A supurb [sic] take-in as ever was got up to guzzle the gullible. . . ."

With that off his chest, Sam could return his attention to his special edition which had been given the grand title *The California Star Express.* Still, with more and more whispers being circulated about the gold discovery, Sam and Dr. Fouregard decided to give it some mention in the special edition. They appended a short item to an essay which dealt with the "Great Sacramento Valley."

". . . California has a mine of gold and a probable estimate of its magnitude cannot be derived from the information we have received," the article cautiously reported. "It was discovered last December on the south branch of the American River Fork, in a low range of hills forming the base of the Sierra Nevada, 30 miles distant from New Helvetia. It is found at a depth of three feet below the surface, and in a strata of soft sand rock. . . ."

But in the same issue, with equal importance, the editors told of the discovery of silver near San Jose (Mission) and a copper deposit near Napa.

Significantly perhaps, it was April Fool's Day when *The California Star Express* was ready for distribution. Realizing that the delivery of the mail and papers would be an arduous and dangerous job, Sam hired a leather-seated Mormon, Nathan Hawk, to become the messenger for the overland newspaper shipments. Sam accompanied him as far as Sacramento to talk with Captain Sutter, whom he now found to be quite different from the happy Swiss emigrant he had met not so long before.

"Gold! Gold! Gold!" Sutter sputtered angrily. "That's all I hear. No one wants to work anymore. They are gold crazy." He twisted his wide-brimmed Panama nervously in his hands.

"Maybe you ought to get out and start digging around yourself, Captain," Sam told him in a teasing voice.

But when he reached the store, Sam discovered that the gold discovery was no longer a laughing matter. More and more men were coming into the store to trade gold dust for the supplies they needed. By now the quinine bottle was filled and there was more dust in a doeskin pouch.

Back in San Francisco Sam was now impressed enough with what he had seen so that he began buying up supplies to stock his store just in case this fever really amounted to something. He was considered the spokesman for his town. People stopped him on the street to ask if there was truth in all these wild rumors.

"You've been to Sutter's Fort—what's really going on up there?" they asked.

"Now don't you worry, when it's really something worth shouting about I'll tell you," Sam reassured them all.

Still, after talking it over with Kemble, he decided that his paper should perhaps print something. In the issue of April 22, 1848, *The Californian* and *The Star* finally agreed, but even then Sam, who usually was as optimistic as a lunatic, was curiously conservative as he wrote:

> We have been informed from unquestionable authority that another still more extensive and valuable gold mine has been discovered towards the head of the American Fork in the Sacramento Valley. We have seen several specimens from it, to the amount of 8 to 10 ounces of pure, virgin gold.

Sam had already decided to open another store at the site of the first gold strike at Coloma. He felt that the time had come for him to look over the gold fields himself, not just speculate about them from his store at Sutter's Fort and in his San Francisco paper.

At Mormon's Bar at Coloma, everywhere along the American River he found men had abandoned their regular work! Marshall's mill stood unfinished, a proposed flour mill lay half erected and rusting, ploughs stood abandoned on Sutter's outlying fields, no one attended the livestock.

Dozens of men, most of them bare-chested and bare-headed, stood in the icy water, with a clear mountain sun beating down on them. No one complained. They rhythmically scooped up the river sands, hoping that each would show the color which meant gold. Many of their pans displayed the flitters of gold. Only a few came up barren.

As the little launch, the *Dice Mi Nada,* tied up to the dock in San Francisco late in the afternoon of May 11, 1848, Sam fingered the quinine bottle he had in his pocket. He pulled it out and noticed how the lowering sun made the gold flakes look like the proverbial "seeds of the sun." He jumped from the boat and started up Montgomery Street. Along the way, he met several friends and some others he knew merely by sight. Sam held up the small bottle, then waved to everyone to follow him. Almost without a word the crowd began to follow and to thicken. With growing excitement, they trailed Sam like children behind the pied piper.

Sam's eyes sparkled and his smile grew wider as the throng continued to grow. His stride became longer and faster as the excitement mounted. The others matched his pace until the whole crowd was nearly running. There was a tide of unsynchronized questions. Why? What was going on?

Sam answered them suddenly, sensing that the climactic moment had arrived. He stopped in the Plaza, near where he had made his first blind search for the flagpole.

"Gold. Gold! GOLD FROM THE AMERICAN RIVER!" he shouted.

He waved the bottle above his head to prove the claim. A hundred eyes moved in unison, like spectators watching a tennis match, as the gold moved to and fro. GOLD!! GOLD!!! GOLD FROM THE AMERICAN RIVER!" he shouted. Then everyone took up the cry. The great gold rush was officially started!

7 The Collector

"There should be enough gold washed out of California to pay all costs of the Mexican War," Colonel Richard B. Mason told Sam Brannan following their inspection tour of the early digging sites. Mason, as military governor of California, had been asked by President Polk to confirm the rumors of the gold strikes. When Mason proved the strike to be true with the shipment of a tea caddy filled with gold dust, Polk's formal announcement on December 5, 1848, started perhaps the greatest mass migration the world had ever seen.

"The war costs should be paid many times over if only a fraction of the claims I have seen prove up," Mason added.

While Sam's faith had never wavered for an instant in the richness of California's resources, with Mason's official endorsement, Sam knew a boom greater than his most optimistic dreams had been launched, and if it was going to rain gold he wanted a bucket, not a fork. Despite the growing misfortune which was overtaking Sutter, Sam extended his own credit to the limit. Through his friends and San Francisco brokers and agents, he bought cargoes which he had never seen and were still at sea. Although his stores were strategically located in the gold fields, Sam printed flyers and cards which were distributed to the goldseekers as they swarmed into San Francisco. "Buy from Brannan," they urged, and Brannan's stores became a byword of the mining areas. Everyone knew where they were and that Sam was good for a touch when needed. His grubstakes were given freely and often returned many times their original investment when the miner struck it rich.

Whalers and clippers, after they had beat their way around "Cape Stiff," as Cape Horn was sometimes called, sardined into San Francisco Bay to sidle against a hundred others already idly fretting their anchor chains. Their passengers and crew rushed ashore, but few stayed in San Francisco, just as Sam had anticipated when he had located his stores in the gold fields. At one time there were less than a dozen able-bodied men in all of San Francisco. The school which Sam had proudly helped sponsor and called Marston's School was empty. Half-built houses stood like skeletons in the fog and sun, and the deserted village could no longer support two newspapers. "Gone . . . *The Californian* ceased publication . . . Verdict of the inquest into its demise: gold fever . . ." Sam wrote of the suspension of his rival.

But soon afterward Sam's eloquence referred to the demise of his own newspaper, *The Star.* He and Ed Kemble composed a hasty farewell: "In fewer words than are usually employed in the announcement of similar events, we appear before the remnant of the reading community with the information that we have stopped the paper—that its publication ceased with the last issue. We have done. Let our parting words be, Hasta Luego. . . ."

With the suspension of *The Star,* the entire area of what was to become California was without a newspaper. In time that would be remedied, for Ed Kemble later merged the *Californian* and *Star* into the *Alta Californian,* one of the premier pioneer newspapers.

Having recovered his original modest investment many times over, Sam didn't look back when *The Star* eclipsed. His stores were making $5,000 a day! Oddly, Charles Smith didn't have faith in the future and sold his interest to Sam for $50,000 in gold. Sam was delighted with the bargain and looked for more. One came from an unexpected quarter.

Captain Sutter's land and possessions had been literally stolen from him, and his eldest son, John, Jr., arrived in Sacramento to assist in the management and preservation of the crumbling empire. Sutter was being pressed at every hand by creditors, especially by the Russians from whom he had bought Fort Ross, on terms, many years before. Because William Leidesdorff, who was acting as agent for the Russians, was threatening a levy which would tie up all of the lands, George McKinstry arranged a full transfer of the Sutter property from father to son. While the ethics and legality of this transfer might be open to challenge, it did protect the American creditors' interests, of whom Sam Brannan was one.

Sam presented a claim for $15,000, representing goods and services supplied Sutter and his employees, and the debt was admitted. But young Sutter claimed he didn't have the necessary cash. Sam waved that away; Sutter was land poor, Sam observed, and the land around Sutter's Fort could be subdivided into a thriving city, especially since Sacramento was already established as the major supply point for all the northern diggings. Sam offered to hire a surveyor, add that to his bill, then take 200 lots of his choice in the proposed city. Though young Sutter would have liked to consult with his father, who was in the mountains somewhere, he agreed. Lt. William H. Warner was hired as engineer and Sam retained Peter H. Burnett, who would later be governor of California, as his lawyer. Sam's acquisition of the Sacramento property made him one of California's major owners of city property and it was a long stride toward making Sam Brannan one of the first millionaires in the Golden State.

Sam didn't let the Sacramento property lie idle long. The

less desirable lots went for $250 each, and those along the river front, Jib-Boom Street as it was called, sold for $500. No one tried to haggle or bargain at those prices, and demand was so brisk that Sam limited sales to parcels of four lots to any one buyer.

Though Sam's merchandise disappeared from the shelves quickly, he was buying in such huge quantities that storage space was soon exhausted. He had a long wooden warehouse at Front and Jay Streets in Sacramento, and when that bulged with goods, Sam bought three ships which had been abandoned in San Francisco Bay. He ordered them sailed up the Sacramento River with new supplies, then anchored them at the Sacramento docks to be used as floating warehouses.

Though most of his interests at that time were centered in Sacramento and his outlying stores were in the gold fields, Sam made frequent excursions to San Francisco to see his family and tend to business there. On one of these trips he sold his interest in *The Star* to Ed Kemble for $800. Kemble already had secured the rights to *The Californian,* and the *Alta Californian* became the new paper.

Though he was able to spend only brief visits with his family, Sam indulged all of them, including his mother-in-law, Mrs. Corwin. They all, Ann Eliza in particular, wanted him home, but Sam explained why he couldn't be there and tried to compensate for his absence by denying them nothing except himself. Sam took extra precautions for their safety because he knew, as the *Alta Californian* said: ". . . San Francisco is without proper officers and is in danger of the assassin's knife and fire. It is the duty of citizens to be aware that they are playing an important part in history . . ."

Sam wondered what kind of history would be written about his city when he saw saloons under every tent and gambling halls being frequented by abandoned women, one of whom was described as ". . . sitting quietly at a monte table dressed in white pants, blue coat and cloth cap, curls dangling over her cheeks, cigar in her mouth and a glass of punch at her side. She bet most boldly, handling the doubloons with her blue kid gloved hands . . ."

Gamblers and saloons filched some money from Sam, but more went to his own private charities through which he provided food, supplies and money for those who legitimately needed them. When friends chided him for his reckless prodigality, he merely shrugged: "A candle doesn't lose anything by sharing its flame and it makes it brighter for everyone— including me."

Sam was fully aware that California was vibrant and alive with the errant and the eccentric, a notable among the latter being Charles Pickett, who was usually called "Philosopher Pickett." But apparently he had abandoned his meditative ways when he shot Bob Alderman over some now-forgotten issue. Because it seemed like a cold-blooded murder, the Sacramentans clamored for a trial, and Sam arrived in Sacramento to learn that Alcalde Bates refused to arrest the lanky Kentuckian who was moody when sober and downright mean when in his cups.

Sam said that something should be done and didn't shrink from taking on the temporary job as alcalde *pro tem,* just for the legal proceedings. When the prosecutor quit, Sam took that job, too, and presented the case to the jury which had been plucked from the streets of Sacramento. Unfortunately, it happened that the jury had been entertained not only too well but too often at an adjacent tavern and fell asleep before a decision could be reached. Reluctantly, Sam was forced to release his prisoner, but he made a silent resolve that the next time he was involved in the enforcement of law it would have a traumatic effect on the wrongdoers, for such a thin fiction of law was only an encouragement to lawlessness.

While some of Sam's actions might be assessed as purely selfish in motive, most of his significant actions struck one blow for himself and two for the community. He was particularly concerned with the encroachment of squatters on Sacramento land, not only his but that owned by other responsible citizens such as Sutter, Henry Schoolcraft and many more. "I think we'd better take steps now," Sam said to a cluster of friends. "If we don't, they'll confuse consideration with weakness and we'll never stop 'em. Ask Captain Sutter here. Who knows better?"

The group of determined men, all armed, mounted their horses following a spirited discussion about the squatter problem. Sam, wearing guns on each hip, had a riata looped about the saddle horn as he rode off toward the shacks.

"Ride over there, John, and warn the man to get out or we'll pull the shack down about his ears," Sam yelled when they stopped before the first scantling shack. Even before the warning was given, a tousled head popped from the darkened doorway. "This is mine! Mine!" the man shouted as he shook a fist at the night-riders.

A sturdy timber was the crutch which kept the teetering shack from collapsing; Sam half-hitched his riata to the support, then knotted the other end to his saddle and backed his horse. The timber groaned, then shrieked as it broke loose. Then Sam wheeled toward another wretched hut which stood on the fringe of a marsh butting the Sacramento River.

This time the squatter threatened Sam with a shotgun. "Don't you jerk down my house," he shouted.

Sam ignored the weapon, spurring his horse directly at the man. Instead of firing, the squatter tried to scramble backward. He stumbled and fell, the scattergun firing harmlessly into the air. Sam rode on, pulling down another shack.

"I believe that'll do for openers," Sam told the others. "We'll get official dispossess notices printed and give 'em twenty-four hours to get out or the rest of their shacks will be burned."

Even though Sam's two excursions into law enforcement had pointed the way for an effective government, he turned down a seat in the local government being organized for the Sacramento area. "With Peter Burnett, John Fowler and all

the rest, who needs me?" he said. However, Sam did manage
to get a policy statement—anti-slavery in nature—adopted by
the officials.

Sam continued to buy heavily in San Francisco and Sacramento real estate, both by outright purchase and through option. Soon he estimated that he might own as much as one-
fourth of Sacramento and maybe a fifth of San Francisco.
There was little doubt that he was fast achieving the title
which he had chosen for himself, Caliph of California.

With Bill Howard and other businessmen, Sam drew plans
for a long wharf at the foot of Leidesdorff Street to facilitate
the mooring and unloading of ships. With such a dock, cargoes could be put directly into wagons and hauled away instead of being lightered ashore. Vision of such a structure was
staggering for those days but worthy of the men who helped
build San Francisco, for this so-called Long Wharf was to be
2,000 feet in length and cost more than $200,000!

"When I stepped ashore in 1846," Sam smiled, "I sure
didn't imagine I'd be chipping in with fifteen thousand for
a wharf. What of it? I'm putting the money back where I
made it: San Francisco."

"Yep, you've almost made a penny do a dollar's work,"
Kanaka Davis laughed. Davis' lucid account of the earliest
days in San Francisco remains one of the fine documents of
those days. "You may be the first millionaire already, Sam."

Sam shook his head slowly and said he didn't know. For almost all his land and possessions was bought on time or held
on option and exchanged so fast that it was impossible to pin
down his exact worth at any one time.

"I don't know if I'm first, but I would be first to admit it,"
Sam said.

Ann Eliza Brannan was becoming increasingly restive with
her husband's absolute devotion to business and civic affairs.
They quarreled frequently now, and she warned him that one
day he might stop and realize that he had nothing but his
money. As usual, Sam ended the arguments with a hasty kiss

on her cheek, then slipped on his frock coat and headed toward the door, hat in hand. "Don't wait up for me, dear," he said. "The month-end reports have come in, and when I catch up with those I may stop and talk with the boys awhile."

"Yes, I know all about your talking," Ann Eliza Brannan said wearily. "What you really mean is gambling, drinking and staying out till all hours."

In the San Francisco evening a fresh salt breeze sprang from the bay, and below were the wavering lights of a city astir at night. As he walked, he decided he wouldn't take any part in the constitutional convention planned for Monterey. Business matters were too pressing. There was the wharf dedication for the start of work, a new store ship to buy, and he had to look over a parcel of land two square miles in size along the Feather River—this in partnership with Hank Cheever. John Fowler also had a deal that interested Sam. He had acquired the frame of an old grist mill and thought it would make a hotel, placed on one of Sam's river-front lots along the Sacramento River. Sam was enthusiastic about the suggestion, and before he had stopped nodding his head, he had involved himself for $80,000. It was to be called the City Hotel, three stories high, draped with fine iron work and fitted with fixtures and furniture imported from New York.

It was late and Sam was tired by the time he finally returned to his small office. He put his feet up on the desk and was sipping a drink when there was a knock on the door.

"Come in," he called, wondering who would be making such a late night call. It must be urgent, he decided. The door swung open and he saw two men, one whom he knew and the other a stranger. Sam dropped his feet and rose to greet them.

"Who's your friend?" Sam asked of Amasa Lyman, a Mormon he had known in earlier days. Lyman's companion was an enormous man, his granite face punctured by gray eyes which had the warmth of marbles. His hair was plaited in two braids which fell over his massive shoulders. He was dressed

in coarse, rough clothing with a high-buttoned coat. But
when he finally spoke, Sam almost burst out laughing, the
contrast to his formidable appearance was so great. But there
was no humor or friendliness in those cold eyes. To recover,
Sam offered both men a drink, which was refused.

"Brother Brigham Young sent me," the outsized man
squeaked out in a falsetto voice, after he had been introduced
as Porter Rockwell. "And I have come to collect the money."

Sam contained himself but said nothing as he waited to
see what would happen next. He had considered this gambit
because of the dissensions which had followed some of the
secular disputes.

"I have come for the money," Rockwell repeated. "Where
is it?"

"What money do you mean?" Sam replied casually.

"The money you have collected from the Mormons as the
Lord's fraction—the tithes," Rockwell said.

Lyman explained that Rockwell was Young's personal
bodyguard and was acting as his representative in this matter.
Sam was familiar with the giant's name, recalling that he had
been involved in a killing or two in the past.

"I mean to have the money," Rockwell persisted. "I'm not
returning without it." To reinforce his intentions, he reached
into the folds of his coat and pulled out a long-barreled pistol
which to Sam seemed to have a bore as big as a stovepipe.

Sam looked at Lyman, at Rockwell, then back at the pistol.
He sat down again, temporarily needing the support.

8   The Chairman

"It is the Lord's money you have, Sam Brannan," Rockwell persisted, keeping the pistol steadily pointed at Sam's chest.

"Do you have a receipt?" Sam asked. Rockwell shook his head, obviously puzzled. Sam continued: "I'll turn over whatever money you think I may be holding when you bring me an official receipt."

Rockwell shook his head slowly and admitted that Brigham Young had not provided him with a receipt.

"I'm not talking about Brigham Young," Sam said. "You claim it is the Lord's money; then bring me a receipt signed by Him if you want any money from me."

Sam's calm manner vanished as he lashed out at Rockwell: "No one knows what they want . . . except money. When the Sam Brannan Company arrived it not only didn't have any money, it was in debt. Do you want a share of that? Who got the debt paid . . . the people settled . . . everyone fed and working? Who brought his own press and supplies? Who organized the New Hope colony? Who has repeatedly grubstaked these people? Who . . . ?"

Sam trembled, then stepped boldly toward Rockwell and pushed aside the pistol. Standing so close he could feel Rockwell's measured breaths, Sam snarled: "Now get out of here! Get out, you lout. If I can't put you into the street myself, I'll call some of my friends to help." He turned toward the back room as though to summon aid.

Rockwell and Lyman hesitated and exchanged glances. Finally, the Mormon giant holstered his gun and the pair turned and left without another word. Slowly, Sam expelled a long breath. His bluff had worked. There hadn't been anyone in back to help him and he had been facing a killer.

Sam was not done with surprise visitors, though the next to arrive were considerably more pleasant. A few days later he was bent over his desk when he was half aware that a man had poked his head in the door. "This the office of Sam Brannan?" the newcomer inquired in a familiar voice.

Sam's chair overturned as he leaped to his feet. "Alex Badlam!" he cried rushing to wring his brother-in-law's hand. Not only had Alex come by ship to California to seek his fortune, he had brought Sam's sister, Mary Ann, the children, Alex Jr., Sarah and Ezra, with him. As soon as Sam had them settled in his own home he set out to introduce Alex to the workings of the city.

Alex was able to understand some of the tremendous drive that made his brother-in-law a success when he watched Sam become engaged in a new venture that very first day they went out to see the city. J. W. Osborne, a shrewd China trader in teas, silks and Oriental knick-knacks, had long wanted Sam to join him in a San Francisco store.

Impressed with Sam's energy and initiative, Osborne believed they could make more money together than either could alone. With customary dispatch, Sam agreed and they made a number of oral arrangements—the usual hatband and handshake variety, typical of those days. Sam agreed to dispose of his other stores and concentrate on the San Francisco store. A local store would give Sam more time with his family, and San Francisco was becoming something of a metropolis now. While most of the buildings were little more than large tents, such as the El Dorado and Bella Union, gambling halls, and other packing-box houses, fingers of a few sturdier buildings were probing the skyline now.

Alex was trailing Sam when they rushed off toward a dockside auction later that afternoon. Sam had seen a tall-masted vessel slide into the Bay and believed she carried a full hold of goods from the Far East. He wanted to be there when the bidding began. Sam saw piles of teas, spices, silks, woven chairs and cheap pottery heaped on the wharf.

"This is only a sampling of what's aboard the *Templar*," auctioneer Jim Gillespie said, as he waved his gavel toward the sleek vessel rocking gently in the water. "Who'll bid on these silks?"

Several called bids and Sam managed to buy a few bolts, though he really wasn't interested in that type of merchandise. Sam identified with the miner and the workingman and usually sought what they wanted. But he was shrewd.

When Gillespie offered a lot of Oolong and Tyson tea, Sams' interest stirred. He spurred the bidding, and the cases of tea were finally knocked down for five dollars per pound. "I'll take all you got," Sam yelled to the auctioneer. The other merchants groaned and shouted they wanted some. "You'll get it, at my price," Sam called, laughingly. "If you'd bid high enough you'd have the same chance as I." Then aside to Alex, Sam added, "This business takes money and nerve, Alex," he said. "I borrow one and bluff the other."

As they left the auction and walked about San Francisco, Sam pointed out the rolling hills which had borne only twisted oak and chaparral when he had arrived but which now were sprouting a carpet of tents, houses and some more substantial buildings. The streets, mere lanes of churned mud, were lined with heaps of garbage and refuse upon which monstrous rats fed.

"There are the worst rats in the area," Sam said, pointing to a large tent displaying a sign which proclaimed: "Tammany Hall." "That's where the scoundrels from New York's

Bowery and the Sydney Ducks from Australia meet to plan their mischief.

"A hoodlum named Sam Roberts is the worst," he added. "Something will have to be done if San Francisco is ever to fulfill its promise."

Once they reached Sam's store at the corner of Montgomery and Sacramento streets, they found that some of the items from the auction had already been delivered. Like the other merchants, Sam displayed heaps of goods outside to attract miners, who helped themselves from the selection and paid for the items inside. It saved storage space and a clutter of customers milling around. Though most of the goods were such things as pans, picks, blankets and buckets, Sam made a small display of the silk. "It'll show 'em this is a high-class store," he told Badlam.

As the two of them were admiring the new display, Sam caught sight of eight or nine men in ragtag remnants of army uniforms coming down the street marching in military formation and elbowing citizens out of their way. Stopping at a merchant's a short distance up the street, they pointed to his display of wares and suddenly, as though at some prearranged signal, they darted inside. Moments later they rushed out, some carrying blankets, others shirts and Panama hats. "Stop! Stop, come back and pay for those!" The alarmed merchant flew to his door, but the men were already well down the street abreast of Sam.

"Come back, you thieves!" Sam bellowed, leaving Alex standing open-mouthed while he raced after the offenders. Sam had almost overtaken them when several stopped abruptly and turned. "What's it to you, Brannan? We took nothing from you. Besides you merchants owe us a few gifts for our protection," one said.

"Protection . . . it's more like blackmail!" Sam cried. Before he could throw up his guard, one of the men dropped the blanket he was carrying and hit Sam with his fist squarely in the mouth. By the time Sam had scrambled back to his feet, itching for a fight, all the hoodlums had disappeared around the next corner.

When Sam had wiped the blood from his face and straightened his clothes, he strode resolutely to the alcalde's office where he offered to identify and sign a complaint against the men who had attacked him.

"You're crazy, Sam," Tom Leavenworth, the alcalde, stated. "Why it's worth a man's life to try and arrest one of those Hounds."

"It is worth a man's honor if you don't," Sam snapped. "This is a disgrace. The time has come to do something when a man can be robbed in daylight and nothing is done."

"It may be time for you," Leavenworth said, "but it ain't my time. I've got my own life to consider. Besides the Hounds say they're the only law and order around here and sometimes they're right."

Sam winced at the words as he realized that San Francisco had long outgrown the days of personal justice. Now that civilized society faced organized gangs of criminals, it was time for responsible citizens to band together and organize also.

Even before he returned to get Alex, Sam stopped and talked with some friends to discuss his plan and the urgent need for organized law, backed by the community itself. The response was not enthusiastic, as few wanted to get involved, even though they realized the implicit dangers. Sam was still troubled when he went to bed that night and his sleep remained troubled for the next week.

The crisis he had vaguely feared did not take long in materializing. On the evening of July 15, Sam was awakened by noisy pounding at the front door. "Sam . . . Sam, come quickly!" called Ann Eliza's terrified voice.

Half-dressed, Sam plunged for the door, anticipating some burly intruder. Instead his wife had her arms around a sobbing dark-skinned woman clad only in nightclothes and a heavy shawl; behind her, two small children, similarly half-dressed, clung to her side. At houses farther down the street other terrified refugees were being cared for, while off to the north a faint pink glow lit the sky.

"It's the Hounds, they've attacked and burned Little Chile," Ann Eliza cried.

Moments later Sam's partner Osborne and other neighbors were gathering in the street, where one of the men told them that the Hounds, with their usual excuse of administering the law, had ridden into Little Chile, the Spanish-speaking settlement of the city, on the pretense of collecting some money for the sheriff. The debtor badly beaten, they had turned to looting, setting fire to the flimsy canvas homes, whipping the men and attacking the women. With most of the able-bodied men off to the gold fields and only the old men, youths and women left behind, the drunken Hounds had encountered little resistance.

Sam jammed a cheroot into his mouth and took off along with most of the other men for the South American settlement. There was little they could do except find refuge for the old and sick, for most of the flimsy homes had been reduced to ashes by now and the Hounds were gone.

"We're living in a civilized age," Sam cried. "It's high time to determine whether decent citizens or the Hounds run San Francisco. People are robbed, killed and beaten and nothing is done. Bodies are found every day, and no one cares. It is time to organize and clean up our city."

The men agreed, but while Sam was anxious to get started, the others urged caution and care. Next day, when the *Alta Californian* published a story of the outrage, some of the Hounds appeared at Kemble's editorial office, where they made a mess of the type cases, overturned composing stones and scattered files. As a calling card they left a skinning knife sticking through the newspaper's account of the Chileno outrage.

This time Sam didn't wait for anyone else to act. At the corner of Clay and Montgomery streets, he flipped over an empty barrel and began to harangue the men in the streets.

Sam related the events leading up to the burning of Little Chile. "Men, now is the time to act," he thundered.

Sam's resonant voice and his earnestness caught the attention of the passers-by and snared them into the crowd, which gradually became larger and larger. As the intersection became clogged with his audience, Sam suggested they move to the Plaza where there would be room for all. Sam was once again the pied piper as he led the others toward what he hoped would be law and order. He walked directly to the one-story adobe office of Alcalde Leavenworth where he climbed to the low roof so he could look down on the crowd. "It seems that our alcalde's office is an appropriate place to lay the foundations for American justice," he announced, "but first I have an announcement.

"The Hounds have just sent word that they will not only burn down my house but will shoot me if I dare to cause them trouble. This is their idea of law and order. Is this the kind of order you want?"

A thunderous roar of protest swelled from the throng on the Plaza.

Sam stood silently for a moment, estimating the disposition of the men below. Suddenly he ripped open his shirt, baring a hirsute chest. A vagrant bay breeze twitched about him, blowing his coat-tails as he posed defiantly.

"Shoot me, scum. Here's your chance," he yelled. "Make good on that threat. If you harm me or my family, see how you fare at the hands of the honest citizens!"

The crowd stirred uneasily at the potentially dangerous situation. Some looked about as if trying to spot the assassin. Sam let the drama linger on, then slowly closed his shirt. "Now you've all seen the cowards we are dealing with," he said. "Go home, get your friends and be back here at three o'clock and we'll decide how to deal with these criminals," he ordered.

The throng suddenly shook free of the oratorical cocoon

which Sam had spun about them. With a round of cheers they dispersed.

Sam hadn't underestimated his fellow San Franciscans. Even before he arrived at a quarter to three a large throng was awaiting him and more pouring in from all directions. The men were receptive, and explosive tempers were apparent now as Sam recited some of the crimes that the Hounds had been responsible for. He hammered at the violence, thefts and the racist activities of Roberts' secret society. His talk was followed by that of another respected citizen, then Sam resumed the leadership again. Bill Howard was named as temporary chairman and Dr. Fouregard secretary-treasurer of the law and order committee by acclamation.

"Now here's where you put your money where your mouth is," Sam called. "We'll need money to help those Chilenos get back on their feet."

Sam whipped off his hat and dumped a handful of gold into it, then leaned down and handed the hat to the man nearest him. "Don't get your fingers stuck in your pockets digging the gold out," he urged. "Remember that woman who was clubbed to death trying to protect her daughter from these devils. Give until it feels good."

Other hats joined Sam's in picking up the contributions. Once the collection had been made to rebuild Little Chile, the business of the Safety Committee went on. Captain W. E. Spofford was put in charge of four patrols, composed of 100 men each. Others were named to lead the smaller individual units and a chain of command was established. San Francisco was divided into districts, and watches were set up so that the streets would always be under surveillance by some of the armed patrols.

"To stop this trouble at the source, we must nab the leaders," Bill Howard said after he had assumed command of the Committee. "Sam Roberts is the first on our list. If we get him, some of the lesser lights will be extinguished."

The effectiveness of the patrols was soon demonstrated

when Roberts, along with sixteen other Hounds, was in custody within twenty-four hours. They were held in the adobe building of Alcalde Leavenworth. In deference to the law, Leavenworth was allowed to sit with Dr. William Gwin and Frank Ward in hearing the cases which would be presented against the Hounds. Horace Hawes and Hall McAllister were named as prosecutors for the Committee.

Evidence that many of the Hounds had been reluctant to submit to the custody of the Committee was apparent when they appeared with blackened eyes, puffed lips and a few bandages over other abrasions. Once the preliminaries had been arranged, the Hounds were taken aboard the *U.S.S. Warren,* the only place where they could be safely jailed because San Francisco lacked anything suitable for a prison. While they were aboard the *Warren,* true bills from a hastily drawn grand jury were handed up for all of them. Individually and collectively, they were cited for riot, robbery, murder and intent to kill.

An outsized jury of twenty-four men was selected and sworn in; then the trials began. After two days, the jury returned guilty verdicts for nine of the Hounds. The rest were acquitted.

"Ten years at hard labor," was the sentence pronounced by Leavenworth for Sam Roberts.

The court was noisy and jubilant with its first success and the severity of the punishment. Sam yelled for order in the court, then addressed the assemblage.

"Now that we've decided who's guilty, who will bell the cat?" Sam asked. "It's fine to sentence Roberts to ten years, but where will he spend it? Who'll guard him? There's no jail."

"Nothing except convicted prisoners," someone admitted ruefully.

Faces of the Committeemen wrinkled in puzzlement. No one had a solution. Roberts and the other Hounds began to smile, then snicker. "You might as well free us, Brannan,"

Roberts taunted. "You can't live with us, and it seems you can't live without us, either."

Sam was silent for a moment, then he exclaimed. "That's it, Roberts. You've got the ticket. The ticket to leave. Banish 'em! Put them, all of them, under threat of summary hanging if they return. Yes, we can live without you, Roberts. You showed us the way."

The idea was immediately and enthusiastically accepted. Sam felt a warm glow of pride and accomplishment when he shook his fist in farewell as he watched the Hounds exiled from his beloved San Francisco.

Sam was pleased that the first step to clean up the city had been taken, but then he wondered how many more would be necessary.

9   The Speculator

Sam fidgeted and ran his finger around the inside of his collar as he sat with Ann Eliza witnessing San Francisco's first concert, which featured Stephen M. Massett. Sam could faintly hear the outside city sounds, and instead of listening to "I'm Sitting on the Stile, Mary," he longed to be where the gongs and bells clanged in front of the restaurants and gambling halls. Or drinking a Blue Blazer while watching a high-stake gambling game at the El Dorado at the corner of Kearney and Washington streets. But Sam endured the cultural torture because Ann Eliza wanted him to, and he was with his family so seldom that they were almost strangers.

Sam, as a city councilman now, had been among the first to receive an invitation, which led him to believe that being a politician had its drawbacks. But there were advantages, too. The city fathers, in order to finance some of the civic expenses, began selling "water lots," city properties which bordered the bay and were only visible during certain low tides. These, a few envisioned, could be artificially filled with dirt which would keep the Bay from washing over them. Once filled, these lots would be immensely valuable, but at present they were being sold for a fraction of their potential.

Since city councilmen knew when parcels of land would be available, many of them were bid on before the public was ever aware of the opportunity. Sam took advantage of these auctions and acquired vast acreages of water lots for less than $100 each. As the sand hills were shoveled into the Bay, the newly-filled lots jumped in price. Sam sold one for $16,000 and another for $40,000. He had erected buildings of some sort on most all of his property which he hoped to keep, and his income from rents alone was at least $150,000 annually and this didn't include the enormous profits he made in various real estate deals or his store in San Francisco. In addition, the City Hotel in Sacramento which he owned with John Fowler promised to return at least another $30,000 annually. Sam turned down a handsome offer for his Montgomery Street holdings, which now stretched between California and Sacramento streets. It was there that he planned to establish the headquarters for his burgeoning financial empire and envisioned a building four stories high! Speculation in real estate wasn't Sam's only forte. At times he bet as much as $10,000 on the turn of a card. Win or lose, it seemed to be the same to Sam. At least he never lost his friendly smile or genial manner.

Even though Sam, along with Peter Burnett, had been a moving force in proposing statehood for California, Sam didn't attend the constitutional convention which was held in Monterey on October 10, 1849. Later he would regret missing a part in this history-making, but at the time he was pressed with business matters and in the process of disposing of his gold field stores. Busy buying merchandise for the San Francisco store, Sam was a daily visitor to the Central Wharf, which was receiving huge amounts of goods from the Pacific Mail steamers which could now be warped alongside the wharf. Besides this, he was able to grab up another block of twelve city lots which were little more than a part of the tides. But as the Bay was pushed back, he erected shacks on these and immediately rented them for $500 to $1,000 per month.

Nothing could dampen Sam's ardor for San Francisco or her future, not even the torrential rains which began in November. Sam got about the city as best he could. During the dry seasons, the lanes which served as streets were ankle deep with choking, powdery dust. Now the streets were long, almost bottomless sloughs of mud.

"I have seen mules stumble in the liquid mud and drown in the slime," William Tecumseh Sherman said. "I dread to ride along Montgomery Street because the horses' legs become entangled in the brush and they are likely to take their rider down with them."

One day on his way to his Montgomery Street offices, Sam saw a drunken miner who had fallen from one of the plank walks which had been thrown on the slimy surface to protect the unwary. Floundering in the mud, the miner was on the point of drowning as Sam held out a shovel. When he had a purchase on it, Sam yanked him to safety.

"Take some of those boxes and throw them into the street," Sam ordered his clerks. "People will drown right before our eyes if we don't. Damn the cost of the merchandise."

Sam wasn't the only merchant trying to stem the tide of mud which engulfed the city. Kegs of nails, Virginia tobacco, flour, sugar and even a piano or two were thrown in. When these desperate, expensive measures only partially corrected the situation some wag crudely lettered a sign and posted it at the corner of Kearney and Montgomery streets:

THIS STREET NOT PASSABLE. NOT EVEN JACK-ASSABLE

Though such things hardly added to the dignity of San Francisco, no one seemed to mind. In the first six months of that year, 9,891 men and 209 women arrived in San Francisco, and 800 houses were added to the growing city. Grace

Church was built and Trinity Church wisely constructed its new house of worship out of sheet iron.

The newly arrived goldseekers were often the subject of practical jokes. Leaving the ships at the foot of Sacramento Street, some wide-eyed forty-niners were astounded to see the street sprinkled with gold dust and small nuggets and, dropping to their knees, began to claw in the mud to get their share. The perpetrator of the joke, though it cost $2,000, considered it worth the price just to watch the newcomers wallow in the mud after the "salted" gold.

Sam didn't like to admit any flaw in San Francisco, but the condition of the streets made even the simplest traveling difficult. Worse than that, thugs and hoodlums were again ranging through the city almost entirely without restraint. Because many of these criminals had lately arrived from Australia and other distant places, the treatment accorded to Sam Roberts was lost on them. Because many were ex-convicts who had served their time in Australia's Penal Colony, they knew no other way of life than crime. Any device was employed to further their ends, and San Francisco was not yet prepared to raise a firm hand against them.

As the Christmas holidays neared, Sam spent more time at home with his wife and children. Ann Eliza planned a simple celebration for them and the two children, inviting only their closest friends and the Badlams.

The Brannans all had a busy day on the twenty-fourth and retired relatively early. Sam slept soundly until he was aroused by the clanging of fire bells shortly before dawn. He jumped from bed and peered through the windows. Below he could see flames leaping skyward in the vicinity of the Plaza, and they seemed to be spreading out of control because of the brisk wind. Within seconds he was pulling on his clothes. He shouted to Ann Eliza that he was going out and that she should watch the fire's progress and direction. "Take care of yourself and the children," he ordered. "If there is a hint of danger, take to the hills. We can always replace the house."

Sam was greeted by several friends when he had reached the fire area. Dennison's Exchange and the Parker House were engulfed in the flames. Osborne, Bill Howard, Talbot Green and many others were trying to do what they could. But lack of water and an abundance of mud made their task impossible. Sam suggested they throw some of the mud on areas where the fire wasn't too intense. But the fire was not to be denied. Sam watched helplessly as buildings, tents and shacks withered and died at the touch of the searing heat, then disappeared in a swoosh of flame.

Once, as the wind changed, sending gusts inland, Sam dashed to the corner.

"Hey there, Jack," he called to a young man who hauled goods for the store occasionally. "Get your wagon and team and drive up to my house. If the fire veers in that direction, start loading furniture as Mrs. Brannan says. But don't let her spend too much time in deciding because she'll want to take everything. Save her and the youngsters. I'll be there just as soon as I can."

The men groused about the lack of rain. "It's been raining buckets for weeks," Howard said, "and the one night we really need it, look at that clear sky!"

Sam realized that there was nothing much he could do and the fire would have to run its course, so he returned to his house, where he found Jack's partially loaded wagon standing hub deep in the mud. Sam ran up the steps to the front porch, then looked back over the city. His eyes flicked from the fire to his wife and her mother, bustling about trying to decide which item was the most important to be saved, then never making a decision.

"Rain, rain where are you tonight?" Sam muttered. Losing patience with the perfidy of nature and the indecision of his family, he whirled about and began issuing orders. "You and you mother stand aside," Sam told Ann Eliza. "You'll never decide on anything. I'll do it."

Sam told them to get their personal possessions and never mind about the household things. "Those can be replaced," Sam declared. "You'll have to hurry. The fire is moving this way."

Sam walked back to the porch and saw that the flames had made considerable progress. He then ordered Jack to load his wife and family into the wagon and get them out of danger. "I'll be along later," Sam called, after he had kissed them goodbye. "Just take care of yourselves."

They had disappeared into the gloom and Sam was back watching the fire when he felt a change in the wind. As quickly as the flames had rushed up the hill, they turned and headed back toward the waterfront. Sam's house had been spared but the flames still raged unchecked. Gunpowder was brought in and buildings in the path of the fire were blown up. Robbed of fuel, the fire died.

Within an hour or so, the city was merely smoldering but there had been a wide swath of destruction. A few days after the fire, the *Tri-Weekly News* reported:

"The Christmas Eve fire burned every building on the east of Portsmouth Square to the ground . . . Yet last evening a band played, coins clinked and glasses tinkled in the rebuilt El Dorado. . . ."

Sam lauded such civic vitality and urged everyone to rebuild, this time even bigger and better. Sam himself had been a heavy loser in the conflagration because of his numerous buildings. For much of what hadn't been burned had been blown up to help extinguish the flames.

The Christmas celebration was forgotten for that year of 1849. Though the fire-fighters had done their best, the only good thing to come out of the holocaust was the fact that they had proved rushing fires could be stopped by blowing up buildings with gunpowder.

"We must do something," Sam told the members of the city council. "There must never be another fire."

At least San Francisco seemed to learn and improve from the grim lessons of disaster, for along with rebuilding they now turned their attention to volunteer fire companies.

Several companies were organized to drag the unwieldy pumpers to the scenes of fires. Four, six, or twenty firemen grabbed the ropes to pull the engines, and they were led by agile young men—the torch boys—who held flaming torches above their heads to guide the engines along the unlighted streets.

Bill Howard was the first to bring an engine to San Francisco. It had been built in Boston and brought around the Horn. The original volunteer company had been known as the Brannan Company, but when Howard made his gift to the volunteers, the firemen voted to rename it the Howard Company.

No one knows for sure who stole the beautiful engine from its garage one night and dumped it into the Bay. But the men of the Howard Company rescued it, restored it to its shiny glory and continued their good work.

Though gold and glory were the treasures sought by all who came to California, others realized that the land under their feet might be the enduring value.

Sam had always held that view, and to consolidate his Sacramento property holdings he paid the Sutter interests $125,000. But with squatters still a major problem, it was a constant struggle to maintain legal possession of the land.

San Francisco, while also plagued with squatters, had an even more complex problem. When California was wrested from Mexico, a treaty covered all of the titles to the land which originally had been Spanish or Mexican grants. But the deeds were poorly drawn and titles were often clouded. Most landowners knew it would take long legal battles to clear them.

Some San Franciscans borrowed money at the going rate of 3 percent per month and prepared to defend their land. Others simply sold for whatever they could get, largely because their faith in San Francisco or American justice didn't extend to their wallets. Sam's faith did, and he became heavily involved in the land trials. But he emerged as owner of huge sections of both San Francisco and Sacramento: his holdings were so large, in fact, that he was virtually landlord of Alta California.

Sam displayed a portion of his prosperity by buying a fine new home in Happy Valley, situated along the old Mission Road. There the Brannans were neighbors to the Howards and other old friends, and there was sunshine and lush green fields in which the children could play. But Sam's feeling of well-being was shattered early on the morning of May 4, 1850, when the dread cry of "fire" again resounded through the city, the sun soon obscured by great clouds of smoke.

10 The Thirty-first Star

Sam joined the other men racing toward the United States Exchange building where this latest fire had started. He slipped into the bucket brigade line, working alongside the others. Soon his hands were blistered, his immaculate clothes muddied and smoke-stained. As he passed the buckets, Sam thought about the action recommended by the city council. Wells were to be dug and a reservoir was to be constructed so that water would be available in all sections of the city. It had been a fine plan but nothing had been done.

San Francisco sustained a four-million-dollar loss in this fire. No buildings were left in an eight-square-block area which lay between Kearney and Dupont Streets. But the city's ability to arise from its own ashes was fantastic. It is little wonder that the phoenix, the legendary fire bird, was chosen for San Francisco's official seal.

One man, whose restaurant had been completely destroyed, began to rake over the still-hot ashes even before the last flame had died. He extinguished the live coals, set up tables, sheltered them with a canvas roof and before that night was over was serving a long line of people.

Sam had another idea about the fires which had been

bothering him for some time. "I think some of these fires are being deliberately set," he told Bill Howard.

"Sam, you're letting your imagination run away with you," his friend replied. "Why would anyone do such a thing?"

"Loot, that's why," Sam said emphatically. "There has been looting during every one of these fires, so much so that I think they are set to divert attention. Those Sydney Ducks don't own any property, so fire doesn't make any difference to them. Robbery and murder can be covered up in a fire."

Howard nodded thoughtfully. "I hadn't thought about it just that way," he said. "There has been looting all right. But we'll just have to watch and see."

Sam didn't let the rebuilding interfere with a picnic he had planned. It was to be held on a small tract of land which he had purchased in the Napa Valley, across the Bay from San Francisco. There were warm mineral springs at the site, and Sam had plans to develop it into a spa equal to any in Europe.

He intended it to be the Saratoga of California, but when he was telling others about it his tongue got tangled and the name came out as "Calistoga." Sam liked this so well that he kept it as the permanent name.

From the para-military groups which had been formed to patrol San Francisco streets, Sam had organized the California Light Guard, which was the progenitor of the California National Guard. Because of his interest and financial support, it gradually became known as Brannan's Guard. These men were among the honored guests at the first Calistoga picnic. Alex Badlam had been made a captain of the Guard, and when someone chided Sam about his nepotism, he replied with a laugh. "Rank and money have privileges. In this case, Alex has the rank and I have the money."

The guests assembled first at the Plaza, then marched briskly toward the Long Wharf where they boarded an excursion craft which docked across the bay near the mouth of the Sacramento River at a place called "Vallejo's." Chartered stagecoaches rattled them to the picnic area, which was in a lush valley with the majestic peak of St. Helena as a back-drop.

Sam didn't overlook the possibility of interesting some of his fellow picnickers in Calistoga and made a speech pointing up its attributes and future. But no one responded, for few had the vision which pushed Sam on.

He was bouyantly happy at the picnic because his family was all united for even such a brief time; even the Badlams were there. Sam was still very fond of Alex Badlam, Jr., and predicted a great future for him. "Maybe we'll be working together someday," he said as he put his arm on the fifteen-year-old's shoulder. "We'd make a great team."

Sam returned to San Francisco refreshed and ready to manage his affairs again. By now he owned the entire Mont-gomery block, which was bounded by California, Kearney and Sacramento Streets. He operated his real estate office from one building there, and now that the fire had been damped down he began planning for two new buildings on Montgomery. No expense was to be spared in their construc-tion, for they were to be built with dressed stone from China. San Francisco deserved such elegance.

There were four newspapers being published daily in the city now and new businesses were opening every day. Keeping pace with these improvements however, were increasing numbers of robberies and murders. Most of them were credited to the Sydney Ducks, who had formed a colony for themselves, a veritable warren for all of the ex-convicts as they arrived from Australia. Police entering the area were bribed or beaten, but in either case there was no effective law.

Even Sam's bottomless energy and confidence in San Fran-cisco was shaken on the morning of June 14, 1850, when fire raged out of control again and burned unchecked for three days. In the resulting confusion, the post office files were broken open and looted, and looting spread.

One merchant dragged a chest containing $30,000 in gold and dumped it into the Bay, hoping to save it later and prevent it from being melted down.

The Army quartermaster's warehouse began spitting and exploding as fire reached the 5,000 loaded muskets stored there. The fire fighters were saved only because the rifles were pointed skyward. After the fire was over, the gun barrels had been twisted like snakes from the heat.

Five hundred people took refuge on the Long Wharf, which caught fire, isolating them temporarily. Millions of board feet of lumber were devoured, and tons of nails were heat-welded together. Four hundred houses were burned, and surrounding them some rainbow-striped rivulets of molten glass spread on the ground, decorated with bits of broken pottery and crumpled silverware.

The losses were great and one of the heavy losers was Osborne, Sam's business partner in the San Francisco store.

"Sam, this last fire finishes me," Osborne yelled above the din of hammers already busy rebuilding San Francisco. "I've had enough."

"Nonsense," Sam argued. "I've plenty of money and can borrow more. I'll put up your share and in a few weeks this'll be only a memory."

Osborne shook his head. "No, Sam, but thanks for your confidence and generosity. You've got the energy, courage and what it takes to make it big. I'm ready to go back to where it takes less trouble to make a living."

Sam bought Osborne's interest in their business, which was no more than good will because all of the rest had burned. Now he became more outspoken in his charges that the fires were not accidental. Even those which might have been of innocent origin were implemented by other fires, too many to be blamed on accident alone. Sheriff Jack Hayes, an excellent, courageous lawman, did what he could to hold the criminals in check, but faced with public apathy, the sheriff's attempts were merely a stopgap measure. When his friends scoffed at his opinion, Sam decided that he could stand the

repeated losses better than most and they would come around
to his thinking in time.

Saw was also concerned with juvenile delinquency, for he
realized that the atmosphere of a bawdy boom camp town,
which characterized San Francisco as well as many other gold-
mad towns, was no place for young people. They had nothing
worthwhile to do, so they spent their evenings in the gambling halls. Sam organized a citizens' committee to call upon
Dr. David Robinson to see if he would build and operate a
theatre in San Francisco. Taken with Brannan's idea, he
agreed to build the "Adelphi" theatre on the west side of
Dupont Street, between Clay and Washington Streets. The
frame structure was begun immediately and when completed
played to full houses.

Sam wasn't content with just helping the youngsters of
San Francisco. The volunteers of the fire companies needed
recognition and sometimes funds for their "socials." Sam
suggested that certain nights he set aside for the benefit of
the firemen. The famed Kate Hayes was the featured enter-
tainer at one of these benefits. Sam, though he was one of the
founders and thereby entitled to a free seat, paid $500 for
his seat on the night of the benefit. This was the start of
benefit performances for the volunteer firemen and their
families. When the Department was replaced with paid professional firemen, the fund amounted to $150,000.

Sam seemed to have an inborn sense of historical significance because he next set about founding the Society of California Pioneers, which required its members to have been
residents of California prior to January, 1850. Bill Howard
was selected as the first president, but Sam declined any office
because of the press of his own affairs.

Sam had taken out substantial loans in the Eastern money
markets at 12 percent interest to finance his Montgomery
block buildings, which he was determined to make the outstanding block in all of San Francisco. Many of his friends
thought it strange that Sam would have to borrow money
for such an operation. "I have never been free of debt, nor

do I want to be," he explained. "I believe in keeping my money working for me all the time. As long as I keep it on the move, my fortune's prosper. Once the machinery stops, I will be like a clock with a busted spring."

Sam was away from San Francisco buying a large section of land near the town of Marysville when his wife gave birth to another daughter. Named Fanny Kemble Brannan, she became Sam's favorite.

But his fortunes took another turn when San Francisco was again devastated by fire on September 17, 1850. This time a hundred businesses were burned, many barely rebuilt since the June fire. San Francisco wasn't to be denied a future, however, and rebuilding began at once. With the repeated building, San Francisco lost all signs of old pastoral California. No longer did the colorful Mexican clothes predominate. Now men dressed in the dark suits of the Yankees: Prince Albert coats, silk hats, and brocaded vests, some sporting turnip watches attached to huge dog chains of gold and decorated with diamonds large as an idol's eye.

October 18, 1850, was a momentous day for San Francisco when the ship *Oregon* rounded into the Bay and scudded for a berth along the Long Wharf. Her rigging was aflutter with pennants and banners. Her cannon boomed with salutes until their barrels steamed. From the top of the mainmast flew the longest and largest flag of all:

CALIFORNIA ADMITTED

The *Oregon's* bell clanged incessantly and the signal cannon in the Plaza answered the salutes while the little-used guns at the Presidio rolled their smoky thunder.

Sam Brannan was in the vanguard of the throngs running toward the dock.

"California has been admitted to the Union!" the captain yelled through a megaphone. "September 9, 1850."

"Now we are all at home again," one woman breathed happily.

"There'll be no more talk about going to the 'States' anymore," another said. "We are part of the United States now."

It was a time for talk and toasts. No work was done in San Francisco that day, nor any other day until the formal celebration of admission as a state was held on October twenty-ninth.

Colonel Stevenson was grand marshal for the parade, assisted by Lt. William Tecumseh Sherman and General Andrés Pico, the last Mexican commander in California. Behind them came a column of marchers carrying an immense banner which read: "E Pluribus Unum."

Sam Brannan was a special guest of honor because of his contributions toward the building and rebuilding of San Francisco. He proudly marched at the head of Brannan's Guard and later gave a speech to commemorate the admission.

". . . Glorious California has now taken her place among the other States," Sam said in a part of his speech. "Its recognition has waited for a long time but at last it is here and we can all rejoice . . ."

Sam spoke glowingly of the future of California, a gamble which everyone should back to the limit of their resources. He concluded his talk on a theme which was always uppermost in his mind. He pointed out that California was a "free state" and must always remain that way to respect the rights of the individual.

The seven hills upon which San Francisco was perched blazed all that night with flickering lights and shooting fireworks.

A little girl, Mary Elizabeth Davis, was also a special guest of honor. Miss Davis, only six, was the first Anglo-Saxon child born in Yerba Buena, April 1, 1845.

That evening, Mayor John Geary opened the grand ball with equally elaborate ceremonies. Mr. and Mrs. Sam Brannan led the grand march, and there wasn't a prouder couple in all of San Francisco, California, the thirty-first state of the Union.

11 The Agreement

"We are pleased to see that each succeeding steamer is bringing to California the wives and families of our merchants and mechanics who have preceded them and built for them a home amongst us," Sam real aloud from the *Alta Californian* as he and his wife enjoyed a leisurely breakfast. "It looks civilized and Christianlike to see ladies daily passing along our streets, amusing themselves in that never-ending occupation of shopping . . . We hope soon to see a society established in San Francisco . . . ."

"I certainly agree," Ann Eliza said. "There's hardly any society fit for genteel folks. There are so many common people about."

Sam hid his smile behind the newspaper. Ann Eliza hadn't changed a whit over the years, proud, haughty, unrelenting. But he shrugged and teased her. "Here's stuff for the grand dame society." He read aloud some of the advertisements which listed blaze and bronze kid boots, Jenny Lind ties, chatelaines and reticules. . . .

"Oh you." Ann Eliza pouted and snatched the newspaper. "Then here's something for you: Colt's revolver for forty dollars, Sazerac brandy, Black Warrior champagne."

Still smiling after the brief but friendly exchange, Sam stepped from the house into the brisk February weather. He and Ann Eliza had been growing more distant over the years, and such friendly moments were becoming rare in the course of their marriage. Ann Eliza had been very upset with the results of the December fire, though was somewhat mollified by the newspaper article which said:

". . . We know that one of the heaviest property owners in the vicinity of the fire—Samuel Brannan, Esq.—voluntarily went to the Mayor and authorized him to take down the entire row of buildings on Montgomery Street to prevent the fire from spreading . . ."

Sam recalled that Ann Eliza had been most pleased with his being called "Esquire" in the article. He also knew her happiness would be fleeting when he stayed downtown with the boys again that night.

But Sam didn't know that the night of February 19, 1851, was to be such a momentous one.

As old Charley Jansen was about to close his small store at the corner of Montgomery and Washington Streets, two young men entered. Jansen walked toward them, noticing that one man was slim, bearded, and hawk-faced, with a long scar on his cheek.

Suddenly, the pair drew guns. "Give us all of the gold or we'll kill you."

Startled by the demand, Jansen stepped back involuntarily, his foot catching on a loose board. To break his fall, he threw up an arm. The thugs apparently thought he was reaching for a weapon and jumped on him. One brandished a slung-shot (a leathern bag filled with sand), and began beating Jansen on the head.

The old man slumped to the floor, his head bloody, his eyes closed while the hoodlums rifled the strong box, finding nearly $2,000, along with a gold watch and a ring which Jansen had taken in as trade for goods. Jansen's wife, roused by the commotion made during the struggle, found her unconscious husband and ran into the street crying for help.

Sam Brannan, Bill Howard, Talbot Green and several others were playing cards when a friend of Sam's rushed in with the news. They threw down their cards and rushed to Jansen's aid. They talked with Mrs. Jansen and heard the old man gasp out a vague description of one assailant. Sam talked over the matter with Colonel Stevenson and both decided that there was little use in trying to apprehend the thugs that night, but Sam hurried to a print shop and had posters run off. They gave the best possible description of the men and asked for any information. Next day, the *Alta Californian* roared:

". . . How many murders have been committed in this city within a year? And who has been hung or shot or punished for any of these crimes? Nobody! How many men shot, stabbed, knocked down and beaten? And who has been punished for these crimes? How many thefts and arsons, robberies and crimes or less note; and who are the perpetrators? . . ."

Within a few days, two men had been taken in custody. One gave his name as Robert Winfred and the other as Thomas Burdue. Both denied any knowledge of the Jansen crime.

The men had been arrested by an off-duty police officer from Sacramento who happened to be in San Francisco during the time of the Jansen crime. He arrested Burdue in the belief that he was actually "English Jim" Stuart, a man accused of murdering a Marysville sheriff and who had broken out of jail before the trial, just a short time before the Jansen affair. Winfred was arrested as an accomplice.

Thus began one of the weirdest cases in criminal annals.

Both men were taken to Jansen's hospital bed where he positively identified Burdue as one of his assailants. But Jansen was less certain about Winfred, though the merchant admitted he resembled the other man.

Search of the men had turned up a gold watch and gold

ring similar to those known to have been taken from Jansen, along with some $338 in gold coin and a bank deposit slip seemingly showing where the rest of the loot had gone. That would be enough to convict him for the Jansen crime. But even more important was to establish Burdue as the wanted "English Jim" Stuart.

Carefully the officers compared physical characteristics: both were the same height and complexion. Both had black beards and a bald spot on their crowns, long wavy hair, ebony black eyes, a scar on the left cheek, a tattooed ring of India ink on one finger, and a stiff finger on the same hand. Coincidence? Impossible! Burdue had to be Stuart.

San Franciscans were in a poisonous mood. An angry mob of more than five thousand assembled in front of the city buildings, and there were yells of "Hang them! Hang them!"

Mayor John Geary mounted a second-story balcony and counseled moderation and reason, warning also against any further attempt to forcibly remove them from jail by pointing to 250 California and Washington Guards who had been called to keep order.

By ten the next morning, when the prisoners' pleas were to be heard, an even larger crowd had assembled. It was the general opinion that Burdue and Winfred should be tried later that day by a selected judge and jury, but Sam, who had held his temper in check, leaped up.

"I am very surprised to hear talk of grand juries and recorders and drawn out trials. I'm tired of such talk. These men are murderers, and I will die or see them hung by the neck. I'm opposed to any further farce in this business. We've had enough of that eighteen months ago when we allowed the convicted Hounds, Sam Roberts and the rest, to be exiled. We are the mayor, the recorder, the hangman and the law. The laws and courts never hung a man in California yet, and every morning we are reading of fresh accounts of murder and robberies. I want no technicalities. Such things are devised to shield the guilty. . . ."

A tremendous roar of approval answered his appeal, though one observer remarked, "Even at that the crowd is probably more temperate than Brannan."

While Sam held the center of attention with his talk, a handbill had been circulated among the mob. It was signed by W. H. Jones, E. H. King, J. B. Huie and S. Brannan. It read:

CITIZENS OF SAN FRANCISCO

"The series of murders and robberies that have been committed in this city seem to leave us entirely in a state of anarchy. When thieves are left without control to rob and kill, then both the honest travelers fear each a thief. Law, it appears, is but a nonentity to be scoffed at. . . .

"All those who would rid our city of robbers and murderers will assemble on Sunday, at two o'clock, on the Plaza."

With a delay in the next meeting, time had a way of assuaging the passions which might have flamed if Sam Brannan had urged overt action at that time. Sam, though known for his militant advocacy of prompt action as a crime deterrent, didn't want the mob to rule but rather a council of twelve men to dispense justice according to the conditions and customs of that day. But Sam's idea of justice for these men was to give 'em a fair trial, then hang 'em.

There was a great crowd gathered in front of the Graham House, at Kearney and Pacific Streets, most of them with sidearms, that Sunday. It was at this time William Coleman, a young lawyer late of Kentucky, stepped forward:

"In deference to Mr. Brannan's well-earned leadership," Coleman said as he mounted the porch, "I say this: We will not leave the matter of justice to the prevailing courts. The people have lost confidence in them and, as suggested, I propose we form an orderly system ourselves. Prisoners can be brought before it, assigned adequate counsel, and testimony heard. If the prisoners are found innocent, they will be released. If guilty, let them be hung as high as Haman before the next sun goes down."

"Why wait with the two men we already have?" Sam asked petulantly. "They answered the description and even Jansen identified them. What more evidence is needed?"

Coleman's calm logic quieted the crowd somewhat, and a committee was formed by acclamation. Howard, Coleman and Brannan were all included. The first public action of the committee was to approve Coleman's suggestion that a trial be held. "All right. We have a committee now, but if this doesn't deal with crime in a summary fashion, there will be a lynch mob to deal with the next hoodlums caught in the act," Sam announced with an air of finality.

Burdue and Winfred were brought before the committee's tribunal. Hall McAllister and Judge Shattuck were appointed counsel for the two men. Foreman of the jury was R. S. Watson, and Coleman assumed the role of public prosecutor.

The key to the defense was the identification of Burdue by Jansen. The defense was able to convince the jury that the grievously wounded Jansen in a large room lighted by only one candle could not make a valid identification. The jury was given the case after a lengthy argument. They deliberated for several hours before announcing that they were hopelessly deadlocked. Nine were for conviction and three for acquittal.

"This is typical of what happens when the courts tinker with justice," Sam growled when a decision to dismiss the hearing was announced. "The shame of it will be on your heads."

Burdue and Winfred were again remanded to the custody of the sheriff, and another trial date was set. Since Jansen had miraculously recovered, they now faced only a robbery and assault charge. Jansen was still firm in his identification of Burdue but uncertain about his companion. As a result of this retrial both men were sentenced to fourteen years in prison. While waiting final disposition of the case, Winfred made his successful escape by digging his way out of his cell, and a short time later Burdue was removed to Marysville to stand another trial there for murder of the sheriff.

Temporarily, at least, the case appeared closed when on May 3, 1851, smoke clutched San Francisco again and the fingers of still another great fire reached through the streets, melting and withering whatever it touched.

The bell atop the Monumental Fire Company house clanged, and Sam raced along with the other members of the Howard Fire Company to fight the fire.

"This is a bad one. Worse than the one we had a year ago," Sam cried, as they reached the fringes of the fire. "San Francisco will go up in smoke. Nothing'll be left!"

Sam's estimate was high but not too far off, for more than two thousand buildings were destroyed with a total loss of $12 million dollars.

The fire had started in a paint shop next to the American House. All of the adjacent buildings quickly whooshed up in flame, and the fire spread with startling rapidity because the flames moved through the man-made tunnels formed by planks laid down as walkways along the streets. Built in interlocking series, the sidewalks acted as chimneys to suck the fire from one place to another, without anyone being aware of it until flames erupted blocks away.

Three men were roasted alive in the Wells Fargo building.

One man fell dead on Washington Street from overexertion.

At five o'clock a man on Jackson Street between Kearney and Dupont shot a fatally burned woman to death, then turned the gun on himself.

Sam and Bill Howard led a throng to the wharf and dock areas. On the way, they helped throw more than $1 million in gold specie down a well to prevent it from being melted down in the intense flames.

DeWitt and Harrison, lacking any water to save their buildings, used 80,000 gallons of vinegar to wet down the flames and save their warehouse.

"Get boats and axes," Sam yelled when they reached the wharf. He helped men shove off from shore to reach the wharf behind the flames, where they chopped the pier in two to prevent the flames from burning it all. Their action saved much of the wharf, but the portion closest to shore was only a cluster of gaunt, blackened sticks.

The fire was so widespread and enormous that an image of the ravaged city was reflected in the sky. People as far away as Monterey, almost a hundred miles to the south, could see the terrifying panorama of a city in flames.

The *Niantic*, an abandoned vessel which Kanaka Davis had beached, then refitted as a hotel, was burned to a shell. Howard and Green, the merchants, were burned out, too. The water being played on the fire turned to steam before it quenched the flames.

Once more Sam suffered staggering losses. Some of his buildings were burnt; others were blown up to control the blaze. But his far-flung empire was still sound and served as collateral upon which he could borrow more money. And Sam needed lots of money to spark his businesses, for he also offered to help Howard and Green get started again. "We're all hard hit, Bill," Sam said to his friend. "But San Francisco and California have no limits to their futures. We can all make it back together."

Howard agreed. "If we had what the Sydney Ducks looted during the fire, none of us would want." He also confirmed the suspicion that Sam had long held.

"Well, the next time we have a pair of thugs in custody, I hope it's them not the jury that is hung," Sam commented bitterly.

"The fireproof building of Gibbs and Company on the Long Wharf was but slightly injured by the whirlwind of flames that surrounded it," read a story in the San Francisco *Picayune*. "Its escape from destruction is a powerful argument in favor of fireproof buildings."

People heeded this advice and many of the new buildings were constructed with brick, adobe and even metal, and within a month San Francisco showed astounding progress in its rebirth. Wagons loaded with building materials moved slowly through the streets and the sounds of construction were again heard everywhere.

It was a quiet, sunny June morning when the Brannans prepared to attend Episcopal Church services. As they left the house, the ominous sound of the Monumental bell clanged. Without a sword Sam dashed back into the house, stripped off his frock coat, flung away his silk hat and donned an old jacket suitable for the dirty work ahead. "When will those fires ever stop?" he muttered. "Something has to be done."

Because all of the business district had already burned out, this fire found its fuel in the outlying homes. Sixteen square blocks were leveled, including many of the old landmarks recalling the Yerba Buena days. The courage of some of the pioneers melted in the fire. Tom Maguire, impresario of the Jenny Lind Theatre, despaired of a future in San Francisco, for he had rebuilt his fire-gutted show house six times.

"The fire started in some shacks I own," Colonel Stevenson told Sam. "A miner named Ben Lewis came home and fell asleep without turning off his lamp. Must have flipped over during the morning sometime."

"These things have been happening too often and too accidentally," Sam said. "Let's take this Lewis into custody until we make sure of all the facts."

Stevenson agreed with Sam that arson might well be at the bottom of these repeated fires. "Arson and looting, what a combination," the Colonel said.

"It is long past the time that something should have been

done," Sam growled. "We should have formed a law and order committee when we tried Burdue and Winfred. One that would have worked," he paused, "and I think the time has come when the rest of San Francisco may agree with me."

Stevenson nodded, waiting for Sam to suggest the next move.

12 Lay Hold, Lovers of Liberty

Though June 8, 1851, was a Sunday, Sam was seated before the roll-top desk in his Montgomery Street office. Restive about recent events and unable to share his anxieties with Ann Eliza, he had decided to work to ease his restlessness. Near at hand was a bottle of brandy and a glass.

Ben Lewis, taken in custody as responsible for the last fire, had escaped from the lax San Francisco police. That had been annoying enough, but Sam learned that Lewis had been arrested previously, had broken out then, and had openly bragged that he would set all of San Francisco on fire. It was apparent now that he had made good his threat. Once Lewis was safe within the warrens of the Sydney Ducks, the criminals issued a public warning that if there were any more arrests or if the police harassed them, they would set fire to San Francisco again and again, until nothing remained! Sam was worrying a drink and turning these matters over in his mind when his thoughts were suddenly interrupted by a knock on the door.

"Good to see you," Sam said as he shook hands with George Oakes and Jim Neall, both San Francisco merchants.

"What brings you around? How did you even know I'd be here?"

Oakes said that Mrs. Brannan had told them where Sam might be, then he handed Sam a copy of the *Alta Californian* with an article marked. "This is really what brought us, Sam. This editorial, 'Propositions for the Public Safety,' says just about what you have been telling us for months. Guess I had to see it in print before I'd believe it. But I agree now, the time has come for some action—like you suggested."

Sam smiled broadly and called to his clerk, Wardwell, to take notes of their discussion.

"Well, I hope others are coming to their senses, too," Sam said. "We have taken a terrible financial beating, and it has to stop."

It was apparent to all of them that a public meeting was necessary to get the backing needed. Oakes said he would arrange to clear the California Company Firehouse for the meeting, and together they phrased a letter to be sent to all of the responsible business and professional men in San Francisco. Special letters also went to such men as Mr. Agenti, who had been paying for a private patrol to guard his property, and Captain Hunter, skipper of the revenue cutter *Polk,* who had occasionally sent shore patrols to clean up the worst dives of the Barbary Coast. Having already made sporadic attempts at law and order, they should welcome a concerted action from all of the responsible people in San Francisco to put the criminals down once and for all.

Even before this public meeting could be assembled, one of the local magistrates made a startling decision which pointed up the dire need for honest government. Judge Parsons quashed any charges against Lewis, approving and lauding his escape! Parsons then disqualified the grand jury, which meant that there was no restraint until a new jury was organized. It was practically a license to kill and rob until the first of July, when a new grand jury would sit. When William Walker, a feisty newspaper editor, flayed the

Judge in print, Parsons ordered Walker jailed for contempt of court. Public pressure got Walker free but the issues were even more clearly drawn now.

Forty men, all disgusted and angry, attended the first meeting sponsored by Sam and the others. Sam, Oakes and Neall agreed that there was no use in haranguing these men because they all knew too well what crimes had been perpetrated. After a brief organizational session, they adjourned until a second meeting that night.

"We'll draw up some general rules of conduct," Sam said as the meeting was closed. "Then the committee will have some definite guidelines."

More than one hundred men returned that evening to the meeting which was held in Sam Brannan's office. Though there was a surface air of geniality and friendship, underlying it was a feeling of tension and of grim determination.

"The proposed document is here for your consideration," Sam said to the assembled men. "We'll have an open discussion as to necessary changes.

"Basically we have agreed that we will all support established law enforcement whenever it shows responsibility in dealing with crime and punishment. Agreed?"

There was a hum of approval and nods.

The name "Committee of Vigilance" was adopted after some discussion, though a few favored the Secret Committee and Committee of Safety.

Since no lawyers had been available in composing the documents, there was a certain vagueness, but they pledged to mutually protect lives, fortunes and honor.

"But here's the real crux of the thing," Sam said as he continued to read: ". . . we are determined that no thief, burglar, arsonist or assassin shall escape punishment, either by quibbles of law, the insecurity of prisons, the carelessness or corruption of the Police, or the laxity of those who pretend to administer justice . . ."

There was a roar of approval with the reading of this intention, and the whole document was approved by acclamation. The charter was then copied into an account book, eight by ten inches in size, containing ruled, pastel blue pages. Below the charter, the men signed the register.

Selim E. Woodworth was the first man to write his name. He was a relatively young man, having come to California in 1847.

Sam Brannan was the second man to sign the register.

George Oakes was Number 5. He was a commission merchant.

Colonel Stevenson signed with such a bold flourish that it took two lines in the register and no one could be Number 19. Stevenson was one of the oldest and wealthiest residents of San Francisco, and when he finally decided upon overt action against the criminal elements, the clean-up became a thoroughly popular issue. Sam was chosen president of the Committee and "Lewis" was adopted as their password.

Even while the book was being signed, events were taking place in another part of the city which would give real significance to their Committee of Vigilance.

George Virgin, a shipping company agent, came ashore on the Embarcadero, then walked briskly toward his office on the second floor of a waterfront building. He carried more than a thousand dollars in cash, having just collected a fee from a customer. Virgin kept money in a strong box during the day, since he had no safe in his office, but at night he usually transferred the day's receipts to a big safe located in the saloon on the first floor. Tonight he put his money in the saloon's safe as usual, then went upstairs to see if everything was all right.

Unknown to Virgin, a heavily muscled young man watched his movements. The man, who later said his name was Jess Simpton, stood in the shadows of a doorway. Moonlight bathed the Contra Costa hills but only deepened the shadows in the building recesses where Simpton waited. Though Simpton had previously cased Virgin's routine, he wasn't aware that the day's cash was put in the saloon.

Simpton had stumbled onto this bonanza by accident. He had been in Virgin's office inquiring about shipping rates when he spotted the cash box stuffed with money. To confirm his plan, Simpton checked Virgin's movements for several days. Simpton thought it would be incredibly easy to walk in, scoop up the money box, put it in a sack, then scuttle back to Sydneytown where he would be safe from any police officer.

Now Simpton watched as Virgin went into the building, then after a time, reappeared heading away from his office, apparently homeward bound. As soon as he had disappeared into the night, Simpton scuttled up the stairway and applied a pinch bar to the door of the office. The oak door had a stout lock and it took him longer than expected. He had to be particularly cautious as there was a light showing in the adjoining office. Finally the door was forced and Simpton swung his torch in the gloom. He spotted the cash box and dropped it into a gunny sack, still unaware that it was empty. Simpton strode quickly from the office and was on his way down the stairs when he saw Virgin returning.

Simpton thought fast and nodded in a friendly fashion just as though he knew Virgin, then increased his pace as he skittered down the steps.

Virgin's face crinkled in puzzlement at the nod from the man carrying a bulky sack. He couldn't seem to remember him. It took him just a moment to see the forced door, note the missing box and realize what had happened. He ran from the office and down the stairs, taking several at a time. "Stop thief! Stop thief!" he yelled.

A couple of men ran out of the saloon and took up the chase. Simpton jumped into a skiff which he had previously tied to the Wharf and began frantically rowing. Virgin, Ed Eck and some others commandeered other boats and went after him. Simpton didn't get far in the Bay before he was overtaken. Before his pursuers could stop him, Simpton threw the heavy box over the side, hoping to destroy the damning evidence against him.

Simpton got pretty well roughed up after they reached land because he struggled to free himself. Some ran off looking for police. But Simpton's luck had completely vanished, it seemed. The man who took charge of Simpton had just signed the Vigilance register as Dave Arrowsmith, Number 25. And he was being helped by George Schenck, Number 72. Between them, they decided that this was a case for the Committee of Vigilance to consider.

Oakes, Sam and a few of the Committee were still at Brannan's office when Simpton was dragged in. Indeed they did want to see Simpton! Others would too! One of the committeemen left, and soon afterward the bell atop the Monumental Fire House began to toll: two strikes, pause, two strikes, pause, two strikes.

Eight committeemen responded to the bell's toll. There would have been more but many later said they didn't know what the bell meant, and others claimed they didn't hear it. Simpton was securely tied and placed in another room while the Committee decided just what they should do.

"Maybe we should turn him over to the police," one member suggested.

"No! No!" Sam shouted. "That will just compound old errors and he will be set free. If we are ever to stand on our own, this must be the time."

Even while they were still discussing the proper course to take, one of the men brought in the dripping gunny sack, which still held the strong box. There would be no lack of proof now because of the many witnesses who had seen Simpton throw the box over the side. Yet there was still some uncertainty among the members because they didn't quite know what to do with the power they had voted themselves. Sam recognized Bill Howard, who had signed as Number 17.

"We are assembled here to hang somebody," Howard said gruffly. "I say, let's do it and give these criminals their first lesson."

Sam Brannan shouted approval. "That's the way to talk, Howard." He rapped for order, "But our articles call for a trial for every accused man. Let's get on with that first."

As president of the Committee of Vigilance, Sam presided over the meeting. Schenck was appointed as prosecutor and Simpton chose to act as his own counsel. The rest of the assembled committeemen were to act as a jury.

Simpton was his own worst witness. For some reason which has never been clearly explained, he denied that his name was actually Simpton. Instead, he claimed it was John Jenkins.

Such a name for an Englishman or Australian, which he was, was as common as John Smith, and the sudden change of identity made the committee believe that he might be responsible for other, perhaps worse crimes. The change worked to his disadvantage in the minds of the jury. Then Jenkins (the name by which he is most remembered) requested one character witness be allowed to testify. Sam immediately agreed and asked one of the men to go find the witness. He returned alone shortly with word that Jenkins' witness said that he couldn't say anything particularly good about the accused, and besides he didn't want to get involved with the Committee. Sullenly Jenkins gave up any pretense of a defense against the crime. But now he warned that if he was convicted, the Sydney Ducks would soon make San Francisco mightily regret it.

Jenkins next hinted that there would be a jail delivery anyway.

By now Jenkins' arrogance had antagonized even the most timid members of the Committee. As word leaked out of the events taking place in Sam's office, the San Francisco police rapped on the door demanding that the prisoner be delivered to them. David Broderick, a prominent and influential politician, threatened legal action if they took steps outside the law; and the mayor publicly announced that he would call out the militia if necessary to disperse the self-appointed Vigilantes.

Sam Brannan set the tone for the Committee when he scoffed, "That'll be the day. How will he raise any men or money for military company? All of the important citizens have signed our book."

It was near midnight when the jury reached a verdict of guilty and a sentence of death by unanimous vote.

A stout hand pulled the rope for the Monumental fire bell again. Two strikes, pause, two strikes. Brannan went outside to speak to the crowd which had assembled at the corner. He implored the people there not to interfere with the events which were about to take place. They would all be informed as the affair progressed.

"Are all of you back of the Committee of Vigilance?" Sam asked of the crowd. It was a curious act of Sam's to ask for affirmation and approval, but he got a wild cheer in answer. There were also a few strident "no" voices but they were quickly shushed down. A voice from the crowd asked Sam to identify himself.

"I am Sam Brannan and president of the Committee of Vigilance," he answered with a note of pride.

"Who are the others?" the anonymous questioner persisted.

"You have my name, that's enough," Sam shouted. "You'll have no others from me."

William Coleman was again urging caution in the hanging of Jenkins. He suggested that the hearing and verdict be set over until there was less passion involved. But the Committee was in no mood to listen to any voice of moderation. Jenkins, in sudden desperation, became so foul-mouthed in his abuse of the Committee and his threats that even the moderate Coleman dropped his plea for mercy or delay.

At first Jenkins refused any spiritual counsel, but the Rev. Flavel Mines was summoned anyway. Jenkins became more

shaken as he realized that execution was near, and his im-
precations and oaths became even more violent. After nearly
an hour, Mines withdrew, admitting that he hadn't accomplished anything with Jenkins.

With the job to do, Coleman fetched a length of Manila
rope from Watson's store.

"We'll take Jenkins to the Plaza for the hanging," Sam
announced. Some of the Vigilance members protested that
there might be mob action, or an escape attempt somewhere
along the half-mile march from Sam's office to this location.

"No, the crowd is with us," Brannan said. "I have talked
with them. We must not be secretive. We must show them
we are acting openly for the good of all or our efforts will
be condemned." However, Sam was persuaded to select several of the Committee to infiltrate the crowd before the
march, so they could overhear any plans for attack and be
in a position to put down any disturbance. Another group was
sent ahead as a working party to prepare the scaffold. "We
want this to go off like clockwork just as soon as we get him
there," Sam said. "You, Wakeman, Coleman, Schenck, fix the
rope from one of the beams that sticks out from the old
custom house. Wakeman, you act as hangman."

Captain Ned Wakeman, master of the famed riverboat
New World, nodded. He was a man of indomitable will and
discipline and was sometimes called the "Paddlewheel Pirate."

It was a clear moonlight night and near 2 A.M. When preparations were finally completed, Jenkins was placed in the
center of the Committee members, each of whom carried a
pistol, and they stepped as a body from the office, four abreast
and twenty deep. Here and there were spectators standing
along the street, but most of the crowd around the office had
thinned out considerably in order to rush to the Plaza to get
a good view of the hanging. But the committeemen were taut
with tension during the funeral march.

Once they had gained the Plaza there was a half-hearted

attempt by the sheriff's men to seize Jenkins. But when the Committee closed ranks from all sides, the effort ceased. Broderick, "Dutch Charley" Duane and Ira Cole harangued the Committee from a cart which drove along the route, but though Broderick was a powerful orator they had little influence.

When they reached the old adobe custom house, each man went about his duties as though public hangings were an everyday occurrence. Wakeman quickly slipped the noose over Jenkins' head. Another made the proper fitting over the beam.

The moment of truth had arrived for Jenkins. His final request was for a cigar, which was lighted and placed in his mouth. Suddenly the crowd hushed, and even some of the committeemen hesitated as though aware of the enormity of what they were about to do. Sam had come too far along the road of this new form of law enforcement to turn back now. Springing forward, he grabbed the rope. "Grab hold. Every lover of liberty and good order, lay hold!" he cried.

Galvanized into action again, others sprang to help him. It was ten minutes past two in the morning when Captain Wakeman finally secured the rope to the railing of the porch. Jenkins' body had stopped twitching and turned slowly now in the air above them, where it would be left temporarily as an object lesson to other criminals. The Committee of Vigilance had brought a new brand of law to San Francisco.

13   Never Look Back

The late John Jenkins was still lying in the dead house when a coroner's jury was hastily convened to affix blame for the hanging. David Broderick, a dynamic Irish immigrant who was on the rise as a political power in California second only to Senator William Gwin, had seized upon the public hanging as a political issue. He named Sam Brannan as partially if not wholly responsible for the lynching.

Boldly the *Alta Californian* sided with the Vigilantes and wrote: "No man need be afraid to let his children know that he took part in that transaction. The trial and conviction of Jenkins was not the act of an inflamed and excited mob. His case was fully adjudged with calmness and deliberation, his guilt fully established. . . . Who shall dare judge the Committee? We dare not . . ."

Sam was supremely confident as he walked toward the city buildings where the inquest would be held. The Committee was small but very well organized, and their decisive action had given them greater influence than their numbers would indicate. Best of all, the Vigilantes had the complete support of all the newspapers along with widespread public support. Broderick, a hypnotic orator and titular head of the "Law &

Order Party," considered the Vigilantes a threat to his personal prestige, and the Sydney Ducks naturally clove to his organization as the only salvation they could see.

Sam had been cited along with nine other men to supply information to the coroner. Several police officers and others gave data about the hanging, but their remarks were largely limited to what they had read in the newspapers. Much testimony had been taken before Sam was finally called to give his story.

When sworn, he volunteered his name, address and occupation, then added gratuitously:

"I am also first president of the Committee of Vigilance. If these proceedings have been convened to assess responsibility for the death of John Jenkins, I accept full blame."

Sam's defiant statement threw the coroner off balance from the line of questioning he wanted to pursue, but since Sam had laid it on the line, he went after Sam like a terrier. Confident and eloquent, Sam answered most of the questions but parried others on constitutional grounds. He even managed to insert some glowing phrases for the Vigilantes, observing that they had been organized ". . . with the object to assist the law and administer justice. . . ."

"Yes, yes, Mr. Brannan," the coroner said. "You've told us of your pride and your propaganda. Now, for the record, we would like you to tell us the names of the other Committee members who worked with you."

The hearing room was suddenly silent. Sam studied the faces of the men assembled.

"You have my name, Sam Brannan," he replied slowly, "and that is all you need to know. I accept full responsibility for the Committee."

"Do you realize that we can charge you with murder?" his accuser thundered. "You, and you alone can be held accountable for the death of Jenkins?"

Sam's face creased thoughtfully. He was silent for a moment, then asked:

"If you wanted to hold me, that's fine, for just when have San Francisco authorities ever punished anyone for anything? I'll take my chances in your courts. If I receive just half the leniency of the average criminal, I should be free by dawn. I've been threatened by men more desperate than you, and I wasn't impressed then . . . either."

There were hoots and catcalls from some of the crowd, and the meeting was recessed to consider what action should be taken. It was apparent that the current law enforcement officers had been met on their own grounds and defied. It was equally obvious that if they didn't accept the challenge, the Law & Order Party might draw its last political gasps.

The San Francisco newspapers delivered the mortal blow to the inquest and the Law & Order Party when they next published a full list of the Committee of Vigilance members! The list was composed of the richest, most responsible and powerful men in all California, and it was apparent that the inquest was no match for the Committee. Lamely, the jury announced its verdict, stating that Jenkins had come to his death by strangulation as the result of concerted action by the Committee of Vigilance. Attached to the verdict was a list of the members' names as published in the newspapers. Though 186 names had been printed, for some reason three of the active members were omitted.

Sam was highly pleased with the outcome of the inquest and this public victory of the Vigilantes. The Committee was deluged with requests of men who wished to join the Vigilantes now, and most were accepted. To control the unwieldy group, an executive council was formed, made up of twenty members, most of whom had taken part in the execution of Jenkins. Sam, for a time, presided over the entire Committee.

"There has been scarce a robbery since the hanging of Jenkins," the *Alta Californian* reported in its June 16, 1851, issue. The San Francisco *Herald* echoed: ". . . San Francisco is more free of crime than it has ever been . . ."

Jackson McDuffee, who signed the great register of the Vigilantes as Number 58 and who had some previous police experience, became the sergeant at arms for the Vigilantes and, as such, was the only paid member of the Committee. He was placed in overall charge of the patrols and other preventive methods. His deputies were Van Bokkelen, who was in charge of the city street patrols, and Ned Wakeman, who was in charge of the water-borne patrols. Other members were assigned duties in keeping with their experience, and Sam, as chairman of the twenty-man executive committee, was in overall command.

"You are welcome to the use of my offices and building," Sam announced to a Committee meeting, "but I doubt they will be adequate as we expand. Besides, there are no real facilities for holding any criminals we apprehend."

Brannan and four other Committeemen leased the second floor of a Battery Street building, and then carpenters were hired to partition the room into smaller sections. Sam and the others personally underwrote the expenses of the work plus the $400 per month rent. While they were awaiting remodeling, the Vigilantes continued to use Sam's offices, even though there were now nearly five hundred men signed in the register. With such strength, no politician could afford to incur the displeasure of the Vigilantes.

"How convenient," Isaac Bluxome, Number 71, said as he pointed to the two heavy beams which protruded from above the windows.

The others laughed grimly, realizing the purpose for which these projecting beams might well be used, particularly if the Sydney Ducks resumed their criminal activities.

"It'll save us that long walk to the Plaza, at least," Ned Wakeman said in black humor. "Being a seafaring man, I don't care much for walking."

But temporarily there was little use for the beams, for since the Jenkins hanging crime had not required much of the Vigilantes' attention and they gathered only sporadically to exchange duties and gossip, especially since new members were still coming in. John Sullivan, who had signed the register as 269 and had been one of the men involved during the capture of Jenkins, was assigned to assist Wakeman with water patrols. Another Vigilante, suspicious of Sullivan, wrote a secret memo to the executive committee suggesting that Sullivan was known to associate with people of questionable character and therefore shouldn't be trusted too far.

His record was to have a significant effect on the Vigilantes' ultimate future.

When another fire erupted in San Francisco on June 22, arson was suspected, and Sam gave orders to double the Vigilante patrols to control the looting and offered assistance wherever possible.

Despite the precautions, San Francisco police shot two men who were caught looting. Hysteria-infected mobs beat two other men to death, several thrashed others, and the Vigilantes saved another man who was about to be lynched, proving they were ready to defend as well as prosecute.

Even before the fire had been entirely quenched, Sam met with Bill Howard, George Mellus, Bill Jones and others and all agreed to underwrite a $5,000 reward for information leading to the conviction of the arsonists responsible.

All of the men were rich enough to pay for such information, and they hoped that such a lure might tempt some criminal into talking, if he were provided immunity for himself. Handbills were ordered and men were assigned to post them throughout the city. Meanwhile they resumed consideration of the case of Justo Reyes, a young man who had been caught carrying off some clothing during the fire. Since it was not an aggravated crime, his punishment was relatively light. He was tied to the back of a wagon and flogged with a cat o' nine tails—from which the usual ripping knots had been removed. Reyes scarcely flinched during the whipping, then put on his shirt and left San Francisco on June 24.

The San Francisco *Herald* observed editorially: ". . . it

was exactly the right kind of punishment, and gives proof of the Committee's moderation and good judgment . . ."

Sam was completely confident about the worth of the Vigilantes, though he was viciously attacked in some anonymous handbills which were widely distributed in San Francisco. He paid little attention to the scurrilous attack and the campaign suddenly stopped when the Vigilantes replied in kind by distributing their own announcements. Many residents of San Francisco received gently worded notices stating that a "committee of physicians" had decided that the recipients' health would be much improved somewhere else and perhaps in actual danger if they stayed in San Francisco. Therefore, the bill concluded: ". . . request that you seek a place more congenial to your health . . . by Wednesday next, (Signed) The Committee of Vigilance."

Others received more peremptory orders: YOU ARE HEREBY WARNED TO LEAVE THIS CITY WITHIN FIVE DAYS; these were also signed by the Committee.

Sam continued to insist that the latest fire had been a showdown measure by the Sydney Ducks. "They mean to see if we are determined to run the city, rather than them," he said, proposing a plan which would enable everyone on the Committee to recognize the undesirables. At his insistence, the executive committee hired a photographer (a daguerreotypist) to record the faces of the men wanted. These pictures cost six dollars each (which is equivalent to about twenty-five dollars by modern standards), which indicates the determination the Vigilantes had to stamp out crime wherever possible.

Though they referred to each other as "committeemen," the public had adopted the name "vigilantes," a Spanish word for watchman, and the name stuck. All of the Vigilantes' anonymity was gone anyway, and they were uniformly proud of their work.

When the police still refused to act, the Vigilantes took it upon themselves to conduct a civic cleanup program. "It is apparent that dishonesty is too deep within the police department for them to act," Sam said.

He was a member of one patrol which rounded up twenty of the Sydney Ducks. All were cited on a variety of charges and all were found guilty of at least one charge. Some were publicly flogged, then banished aboard an Australia-bound vessel. Others were simply banished from San Francisco and warned against returning.

The brig *Euphemia,* which had been beached and used as a temporary jail, had been burned in the recent fire, so the Vigilantes dug down in their own pockets and sponsored a new jail which was built and ready for occupancy in only a month.

As the crime decreased so did much of the initial glamor and interest in the Vigilantes. Men began to slough off on their patrol services and it became increasingly difficult to get routine duties accomplished.

But on July 2, 1851, when Jim Adair and Wesley Diggings brought a man into the Vigilante headquarters, things changed. Sam, Schenck and both of the Woodworth brothers were there. The prisoner had been caught in a robbery and Sam studied him closely, feeling he had seen him somewhere before. "Don't I know you?" he asked. The prisoner shook his head violently, denying any acquaintance.

"My name is William Stephens, lately of Brighton, Sussex, England," he said in a cockney accent. "I was born in March of 1819."

"Well, at least that makes us the same age, thirty-two," Sam observed.

The other Vigilantes engaged the man in small talk, and since there was no doubt about his crime, they made no effort to assemble the entire membership.

"He seems willing enough to cooperate," Sam said, "but his face nags at my mind. Let's keep him in store for awhile and see if anything turns up. There is no question about violating his rights since he was caught in the act."

The others nodded agreement and turned back to arranging for passage of some exiled criminals aboard the *Crescent City,* which was sailing for Tasmania.

Though Sam was no longer president of the Vigilantes, he was still a member of the executive committee. For some reason, he didn't believe the prisoner Stephens, especially his statement that he had just come from Sonora, in the southern mines area. His clothes didn't look it. Sam realized that it was flimsy reason but he had faith in his hunches. His suspicions were confirmed suddenly when John Sullivan, the man about whom a secret report had been given to the committee, came on duty for his shift as guard of the Vigilante jail. Looking into the cells to see who was being held, Sullivan gave a startled yell. "I know that man! His name ain't Stephens at all! He's wanted for murder!"

14 Onward

Sullivan's excited cry was answered by Sam and others racing to the cell. "Don't pretend you don't know me," Sullivan said, pointing at the prisoner. "I worked for you for six months at Foster's Bar."

"Who is he, then?" the Vigilantes asked with growing excitement.

"Why he's 'English Jim' Stuart, that's who!" Sullivan announced triumphantly. "He's the man who murdered the sheriff of Auburn. I was there when he was nearly lynched by a mob and he escaped when the rope broke. There's no mistake about it!"

The Committee members looked at each other in stunned disbelief remembering the Burdue case and the man who had been earlier identified as Stuart and sent to Marysville to stand trial. It was a fantastic case of mistaken identity! Was it too late to save the innocent man? Had the man named Burdue been hanged by now? The last anyone knew for sure he was in jail.

Fortunately, fate at its capricious best had taken a hand in the second Burdue trial. There had been one delay after another. Almost at the exact moment when the real Stuart was being recognized, the jury in the Burdue trial had just gone out, with a decision expected momentarily.

What had delayed the trial was not so much the charge of the murder of Sheriff Charles Moore on October 7, 1850, but whether the man being tried was Burdue, as he claimed, or "English Jim" Stuart as others claimed just as stoutly. A messenger was dispatched to delay any action until this matter could be clarified. A verdict of guilty was handed up by the jury on July 4, 1851.

Meanwhile, the executive committee of the Vigilantes swung into action. Four other witnesses identified the man as Stuart, one of these being a deputy sheriff who had once had Stuart in custody.

Faced with his accusers, Stuart coolly called them liars.

Of all the Vigilantes, Sam was the most worried, hoping that nothing had happened to Burdue, for he realized that his impetuousness had nearly cost a man his life!

But it was not only Sam's rash actions which had Burdue in grave peril but the incredible likeness of the two men, for their physical appearance, scars, tattoos, stiff fingers, even the ink marks between two of their fingers were identical! It was a great wonder that Burdue was spared at all.

Stuart was interrogated for seven hours one day. Stuart insisted that he had a relative who worked in a bakery near the Mission. Vigilantes went there and found there was no such person, but learned that someone from the Vigilantes had preceded them and instructed the people there to lie for Stuart.

That wasn't all of their troubles. Frank Pixley, a shyster lawyer known principally for his defense of criminals, was called to look at Stuart because he had maintained during the Burdue affair that he knew the real Stuart. But when hailed before the Vigilantes, Pixley refused to say anything, holding that the Committee was an illegal organization and he would not lend dignity to it. He then tried to get an order

from the court for the delivery of Stuart into legally authorized hands, but the court refused.

In time, the sheriff was impowered to claim Stuart. The
Vigilantes didn't have to refuse the order to the court since
they claimed Stuart was no longer in their custody. He had
been spirited away by two Vigilantes, then handed over to
two others, then to two others, thus making a mockery of
those attempting to interfere with them.

It was more than a week after Stuart had been taken into
custody when he suddenly tired of the game of being William Stephens. "Yes, I am the man known as 'English Jim'
Stuart. I attacked Jansen and robbed him. Not Burdue," he
admitted abruptly.

He then went on to confess to the murder of Sheriff Moore,
thus assuring the release of Burdue. Once Stuart started to
confess, his revelations became virtually a torrent. A catalog
of crime could have been compiled from his confessions, in
which he also implicated twenty-five others. In view of the
length and detail of the confession, Stuart must have hoped
to gain some leniency from the Vigilantes.

"I myself assisted in hearing and reading of the confession," William Coleman said later, "and sat up through the
whole night, and until the morning sun shone before it was
completed. He went through the entire range of his rascal-
ities . . ."

Included in Stuart's confession was the implication of another pair of scoundrels who had long been suspected of
murder and other crimes, but against whom no evidence had
ever been uncovered. These scamps, named Sam Whittaker
and Bob McKenzie, were both in their twenties and both
Australians.

With such a detailed confession, the trial was little more
than a formality.

"You were right all along, Sam," Selim Woodworth said.
"Stuart admitted that they touched off the fires to cover their
other crimes."

When the scope and number of Stuart's crimes became generally known, the anger of the public was excited to a high pitch. A sullen, determined mob gathered in front of the Vigilante offices. Some of these people had friends or relatives who had been killed by the scoundrels known to Stuart. And all of them had suffered from the fires which had been set by the Sydney Ducks.

Even the fact that the Vigilantes had passed the death sentence on Stuart didn't satisfy the mob. Maybe the Vigilantes wouldn't dare take another life as they had Jenkins'. Stuart was disguised with a floppy hat and cloak, then moved from one hiding place to another to prevent an attempted jail delivery. Sam, as he had done before, spoke with the mob and eventually quieted them by convincing them that Stuart would not escape punishment.

Wakeman was to act as hangman again, and they sent out members of the Vigilantes to scout any conspiracy within the mob. More than four hundred of the Vigilantes had witnessed the trial and all were determined men.

"The chairman volunteers to head the procession accompanying Stuart," Woodworth said, as he patted his pistol.

A band of grim-faced men moved along Battery Street toward the Long Wharf where the preparations for a scaffold had been made. They encountered no resistance now that the public had been assured that Stuart was to be hung. The procession moved slowly across Pine toward the intersection of Bush and Market where the Wharf jutted into the Bay. Near the end was a cargo derrick, where Wakeman stood waiting.

Stuart, slight of stature, handsome, bearded, his face calm but mouth compressed, was neatly dressed in a black jacket, white shirt and brown trousers. His patent leather shoes were brightly polished.

Captain Wakeman went about his grisly duties efficiently and it was about three o'clock on July 11, 1851, that the Committee of Vigilance hanged "English Jim" Stuart.

Again the quick execution of the guilty had a salutary effect on the crime incidence in San Francisco, but the Vigilantes were not done. They acted to remove another cancerous growth by apprehending Whittaker and McKenzie, whom Stuart had implicated. Both men confessed to numerous crimes.

Another Vigilante trial was held, and the pair were found guilty and sentenced to be hanged on August 21.

Sam lived up to the reputation he had gained by acting with deadly dispatch with criminals. "There should be no delay in hanging these men," he argued. "Dave Broderick has his political machine oiled and he is fixing to run us over. If we don't hang these scoundrels immediately we'll not only lose our reputation for swift, effective action but we may lose our prisoners as well."

His words were prophetic.

Broderick threw all of his political acumen into the issue. He collared state and federal officials in an effort to restrain Sam's "hoodlums," as he called the Vigilantes. Since Broderick controlled a considerable bloc of votes, he was able to convince Governor McDougal to order Sheriff Jack Hays to form a posse and take possession of Whittaker and McKenzie. Hays, an excellent police officer, took the men by force of arms and lodged them in the San Francisco jail.

The issue of who would prevail was clearly defined and Sam roused the Vigilantes, pointing out the loss of power and prestige if Broderick got away with this. From among the Vigilantes, he enlisted a "jail delivery" committee.

"We will take that jail or sacrifice our lives," several of the grim-faced men insisted.

Sunday was chosen as the best day for the attack, for then the guards were relaxed, short-staffed or resting. Hays was lured away with the invitation to see a bullfight, and the jail, situated on Broadway between Kearny and Dupont, was approached by a few Vigilantes riding in a fine carriage. Earlier, thirty more Vigilantes had asked permission to hear the Sunday services given at the jail and gained entrance that way. When the sermon had been preached and the services were nearing end, the Vigilantes crowded the surprised guards into cells, freed the prisoners and took them into their custody.

Whittaker and McKenzie were escorted immediately to the Vigilante headquarters where ropes and willing men were waiting. Though the jail delivery had been discreet, it seemed that all of San Francisco knew about it, and a throng assembled in front of the Vigilante building.

Without any further discussion, the Vigilantes made ready to use the two projecting beams which Bluxome had noticed the first day. Ropes were secured to the timbers and the nooses dropped over the necks of Whittaker and McKenzie. Minutes later the two men were dead.

To close the ceremony, Sam spoke briefly to the throng below. Sam recalled some of the stirring events which had led to the formation of the first Vigilantes and pointed with understandable pride at their success in dealing with crime in all aspects.

"Here are a pair of confessed criminals," he said, pointing to the dangling bodies of Whittaker and McKenzie. "If we had failed to act decisively, our failure would have put a premium on crime."

The crowd roared their approval.

Not long afterward, with crimes reduced to a minimum, the Vigilantes ceased their active work and the local law enforcement took over again. By that time, Sam was plunging ahead with myriad other ventures, and he took little time to look back on the work which had been accomplished through his somewhat brash but dedicated determination to stamp out crime in San Francisco.

Along with his many other "firsts," Sam Brannan had also been the first Vigilante.

15 Second Committee

Sam was still chuckling as he dropped his copy of the *Alta Californian* and opened the door of his office to welcome Jim Estill, a friend who lived in the Napa Valley.

"You are in a good humor this morning," Estill observed, "and that's good."

"Yes, I was laughing at this account of a lady stroller . . ." Sam reached for the paper and read aloud, " '. . . who was attired in a black satin skirt, very short, with red satin trousers, a yellow crepe shawl and a silk turban . . . followed by a throng of men and boys, the saloon habitués called tavern turtles . . .' "

"That cinches it! San Francisco is too wild for a forty-two-year-old man like you, Sam," Estill said with a smile. "And I have just the place for you to go: the Hawaiian Islands. We can make a ton of money."

Sam's eyes glittered with sudden interest and he carefully creased his trousers and both men sat down.

Estill's plan was for a land promotion using several well-financed men whose names would mean something in the field of speculation. "We can unload the land for a big profit to Californians. You know yourself that people here are used to finding fortunes, and a land scheme will be just the ticket," Estill observed. "Every man here is an adventurer. He had to be to come this far."

Sam nodded, thinking of the dreams he himself had brought to California.

"With each piece of land, we'll include transportation— one way, so we'll be sure that the island is colonized," Estill explained, his voice vibrating with excitement. "With the colony started, we organize a political party controlled by our friends. Then we represent ourselves as the government, petition Congress for protection and get ourselves annexed!"

"Well now," Sam gasped. "You do have a plan, don't you? But I'm not sure I like that part about grabbing control. That sounds like land piracy, filibustering, I'd say."

Estill assured him that there would be no bloodshed, no slavery, the moves would all be peaceful. "You know that feisty little William Walker, the newspaper editor, is talking about liberating all of Mexico."

"Whenever I hear talk about anyone being liberated, I look for the new chains that'll bind the people when the liberators take over," Sam argued. "Too often liberators are fanatics in disguise."

"Maybe so, Sam," Estill said drily, "but what about the Mormon contingent you brought in 'forty-six? They were filibusters of a sort. Armed, drilled and formed into fighting units, even flying a phony flag."

"I guess I never thought of it just that way before," Sam admitted. Reluctant at first, he became enthusiastic as Estill explained the plan in detail. Sam admitted that he would be pressed to find enough cash because of already being spread so thin in other real estate ventures; also he was hesitant to invest money anywhere except California. But, as Estill had anticipated, Sam finally agreed to the venture; its scope appealed to him.

Ann Eliza was furious with Sam's decision to leave San Francisco and gave him a solemn warning that some day he'd return from one of his trips to find his house empty, but Sam smoothed her ruffled feelings by buying her an expensive piece of jewelry and promising her a fine summer house.

Estill and Brannan, along with several other promoters, sailed from San Francisco aboard the *Gamecock* during October of 1851. Sam was carrying about $125,000 in cash and letters of credit, most of it having come from the sale of his remaining interest in San Francisco newspapers. His companions were equally well financed, for all realized that their gambit would require a great deal of money used with even greater finesse.

According to their plan, the men separated when they reached the Islands so as to allay suspicion of their intentions. The syndicate had pooled their money and any of them could draw on it through a San Francisco bank or through an agent in the Hawaiian Islands.

Sam first bought some key city property, then took a tour of the back country, where he immediately became intrigued with a large sugar plantation which was for sale. There were seemingly endless miles of well-tended plants, which flourished along with the tropical flora in the balmy climate. In the midst of the fields, there was an immaculate white plantation house; its baroque gingerbread frescoes reminded him of the fine old homes he had known as a boy back in Saco so many years before. There were sheltering cliffs and streams, clear as molten glass, which cascaded over the rocks. Sam impulsively bought the place without haggling over the price. He already envisioned it as a fine home for Ann Eliza and the children and a place to which he could retire. Retire? He smiled at the thought. The only way he could ever free himself of the enormous responsibility he carried was to liquidate his assets slowly and carefully, else his financial empire would collapse like a house of cards. For all his tremendous wealth, he was trapped in a cage of his own design and making.

In keeping with the scene, Sam, who still loved fine clothes, outfitted himself in a white planter's suit when he spoke to an assemblage of the plantation workers. "There will be no changes, except that you will be working for me, and one day I hope you will be Americans, too." Realizing that he had said too much, Sam tried to cover it with some light-hearted chamber-of-commerce talk about the grandeurs of California.

Sam had no way of knowing if his unintentional slip of the tongue was serious or would be carried further, but he did know that the island king, Kamehameha, was a shrewd ruler and fully appreciated that his kingdom was coveted by all adventurers, who didn't have to come flying the skull and crossbones flag to alarm him. His subjects had been alerted to watch for signs that the foreigners had designs on the Hawaiian Islands.

The syndicate went on buying property and sometimes talking too much. Estill thinly hinted that Congress might have reason to protect American interests in the islands even with force.

"It really isn't any different from the American policy toward California," Sam rationalized. "Tom Larkin, the Monterey merchant, acted as a spy for us. Fremont made a military reconnaisance, then moved in when there was a local rebellion in the Bear Flag Revolt. The control will have been seized before any shot is fired."

They returned to poring over their maps to be sure they had covered all the bases. The syndicate was near the bottom of its ready reserve and even Sam had reached his financial limit. As they discussed their next move, a native interrupted them with a message from King Kamehameha. "I wonder what this means," Estill said. He scanned the letter quickly, and his face darkened.

"We've been asked to leave the Islands," he said tensely. "The King has decreed that we must dispose of our property immediately and get out. Preferably on the next ship!

"That's robbery," Estill exploded. "We'll lose everything. We'll fight the decree!"

To everyone's surprise, Sam exploded into laughter at Estill's frantic appearance. "No, we lose, that's what it means," Sam replied. "We gambled and lost. It is just one of those things that happen. There'll be other opportunities. You can't enjoy the stars if it doesn't get dark once in awhile."

For all his light-hearted pretense it had been a rough blow, especially as Sam realized that he might have betrayed the operation with his enthusiasm about the United States, but he concealed his disappointment, for it was too late to do anything now. He was able to salvage only $45,000 from his $125,000 but satisfied himself with the thought that he was lucky to retrieve anything from the disaster. However, Sam made a solemn oath not to indulge in any more foreign ventures. The fiasco had reaffirmed his belief that California was the only place where he knew what he was doing. But he didn't look far enough into the future. He would have reason to reconsider and be glad that he did.

San Francisco looked good when they returned from the Hawaiian Islands. It didn't seem possible that the city could have prospered so mightily, particularly after being little more than scorched earth so many times. The Bay was crowded with vessels, most of them active in foreign trade again now that the first blush of the gold rush was over. Sand, rock and earth had been dumped in countless thousands of tons to fill the shoreline and recover some of the "water lots." Fingers of wharfs pointed out in the Bay to snare incoming ships.

Sam's favorite thoroughfare, Montgomery Street, was now the bustling, undisputed financial center of the West.

Because of his mounting difficulties with Ann Eliza, who wanted to tour Europe and give the children the advantage of a Continental education, Sam had a small apartment outfitted in the office building he owned on Montgomery Street. He stayed there when working late or when he had celebrated some successful venture too grandly. As a result of the Island debacle, he needed ready money to continue his buildings, which already stood him a half-million dollars. It was during this time that Sam experienced one of his greatest joys when a second son, Don Francisco, was born. Temporarily, Sam resumed his position as head of the happy, noisy home on Bush Street. Ann Eliza sometimes objected to Sam's rough, noisy games with the children, but Sam loved them.

During those months of reconciliation Sam seldom used his apartment, but his daytime hours continued to be devoted to business, including the building of a Wells Fargo office for the fearless messengers of the West, and building an armory where the California Light Guard could drill and hold socials. Sam also founded the Odd Fellows Lodge and donated a large section of city property for a cemetery—the land being worth at least half a million dollars. It was a time of feverish activity and Sam seldom considered the long-range effects of his building. He took each day as it appeared, shook it empty, then turned to the next.

Sam planned a trip to New York to arrange a line of credit which he would need for the bank he hoped to open. By now Sam realized one of his great failings was that of lending money to anyone who asked, without much plan for its return.

While he had no intentions of forsaking his friends in need, Sam knew he should operate on a sounder basis. But a bank required money, lots of it; and he was short of cash. In New York he hoped to borrow money at an attractive rate. With the decision made, he boarded a Pacific Mail steamer, making some haste in leaving because Ann Eliza was planning a grand ball at the Oriental Hotel and he disliked such social affairs.

Reaching the East after an uneventful voyage, Sam went first to Washington where he conferred with California's senator, William Gwin, regarding legislation which would clear the clouded land titles resulting from the change of ownership from Mexico to the United States. His interest in these laws was a vital one because he would undoubtedly be asked to pledge land as security for his loans; and New York bankers would want property without any clouded titles. Once assured of clear titles, the bankers readily extended Sam all the money he wanted. They not only accepted the land at the value he set, but they seemed to have great confidence in Sam himself and he was able to obtain money at about one-fourth of the interest rate charged on the West Coast.

Quite by accident Sam learned that his first wife, Hattie, was now living in New York. Even more surprising, he learned of their daughter, Elmira. He was still trying to decide the best course to take when, in deep thought, he bumped into a man on the street. Sam swung to apologize and his face turned to a mask of astonishment. The man, neatly dressed in the uniform of a ship's officer, was his brother, Captain John Brannan. Though they corresponded occasionally, they hadn't seen each other for years.

After they had exchanged initial greetings, John insisted that Sam come to his home to meet his wife, Mary, and their two youngsters. It was joyous reunion, and as they talked Sam became insistent that his brother and family come to California. He offered John a job as his business manager, at more money than he was making as a ship captain, and work that would certainly be easier. After some persuasion, John agreed, provided that he could make one final voyage to China before rejoining them all in San Francisco.

Sam leased a fine house in New York, hoping that eventually Ann Eliza would enjoy the plush elegance of the residence and the ready access it would provide to New York society.

Though Sam dreaded it, he then sought out Hattie. He found her to be a plump, pleasant woman, not much changed during the many years. He was relieved when Hattie didn't become unduly excited about their reunion or even seem particularly surprisd. He learned that when Hattie's father died, he had left her comfortably provided for, so that she and Elmira had never wanted for much, though they were not rich by any standards. Hattie made no demands on Sam but speared him with a thunderbolt when she suddenly remarked, "Sam, I guess you got a divorce, didn't you? I never got one, but when I heard you married again I knew you must have taken care of it."

Sam blanched at the disclosure. No, he hadn't obtained a divorce, he admitted, but it was far too late to do anything now. Think of the scandal! Think of what Ann Eliza would say! Sam shuddered. No, it would never do to divorce now.

When Hattie said she would like to move to California, Sam for once in his life tried to talk down the glories of the state. But she would have none of it. When he saw that nothing would deter her, Sam offered a compromise.

"All right, if you are determined, Hattie. I have a piece of property up near Petaluma which will be just fine for you and Elmira. It is a lovely valley and I'm sure you'll like it."

Besides being an attractive rural area, Petaluma also had the advantage of being quite a few miles north of San Francisco. With luck maybe Ann Eliza would always remain ignorant of Hattie and their claim on the same man.

Sam, with his mission accomplished and enough surprises to last him for awhile, took passage on a ship bound for San Francisco by way of New Orleans and the Isthmus. He was delighted to find among the 460 other passengers a number of notables, including Thomas Larkin, Senator Gwin, Congressman Weller, and that lovely actress and dancer who shook European empires, Lola Montez, who was traveling with Patrick Hull, her fiancé. Lola was as beautiful as cloisonné china and as predatory as a wolverine. Sam, like every other man aboard, was enchanted with her. Even the *Alta Californian* took breathless note of her arrival!

". . . This lady, one of the world's celebrities, the favorite of monarchs, of Patrician and Plebian, the fearless, the eccentric Lola is among us . . ." She lived up to her promise and carved a niche in Western history. Sam's interest in her was limited to his enthusiasm for the theatre which he had promoted for the benefit of the younger generation. Sam considered it a privilege to pay $500 for a concert seat to hear the notables and other entertainers.

Whatever his problems, Sam's spirits bobbed to the surface again once he was back in his beloved San Francisco. His generosity was unlimited. One day, being in a particularly expansive mood, he rounded up every street urchin in sight, herded them into a store and ordered grandly that all be outfitted with new clothes and shoes. Smiling, he accepted the shrill thanks of all except one small, puzzled looking youth.

"What're you giving me clothes for? I just got messed up in a fight. My pop's as rich as you are," the lad protested.

It was typical that Sam roared with laughter at his misplaced generosity and later liked to tell this tale on himself and the boy's wealthy father. While Sam drew criticism for his profligacy in later years, he was a true philanthropist, giving not only for need but for the sheer joy of giving.

While Sam never denied his family anything, he and Ann Eliza grew increasingly at odds over his public conduct and her aspirations in society. During the first years in San Francisco, Ann Eliza had been satisfied with local social events, but she now considered San Francisco society homespun. New York and Europe were more to her liking. He was willing to buy homes wherever she wanted but he was determined to keep California their permanent home.

"I don't care what you want," he stormed. "Have your tea parties and social functions but we have to have money to finance them, and San Francisco is where I stay to make it!"

Despite the widening schism, tragedy drew them together momentarily.

Sam had sought refuge in his Montgomery Street apartment when he received a message from Ann Eliza: "Come at once. Don Francisco desperately ill."

The frail youngster, only two, seemed lost in the huge

bed upon which he tossed feverishly. His face was flushed and his breathing labored. The doctor told Sam that there was nothing further that could be done medically. If the boy survived, it would be because the fever burned itself out, not because of human aid.

Don Francisco, Sam's favorite, died that night and was buried in San Francisco. In time he was reburied in the Calistoga graveyard, which also contained many members of the Brannan family in later years.

John Brannan and his family arrived during these trying times, and Sam was relieved to transfer some of his complex affairs to his brother, while he journeyed to Sacramento. A lumber schooner had become stranded on Point Lobos and John's first job was to salvage the cargo, which, some say, was used to construct the famed Seal Rocks House, long a landmark of the San Francisco shoreline. Sam indulged himself in the therapy of buying property while he was in the Sacramento area, most of which he didn't see a real need for. But for so long he had watched his investments appreciate that by now his real estate buying had become as reckless as addictive gambling.

Sam was lounging in his Sacramento offices near Front Street when Theodore Judah came in. Judah, a visionary engineer who believed he could put a railroad across the Sierras despite the monumental obstacles, had already won the nickname "Crazy Judah." But he had a preliminary scheme now, one which he believed Sam might see fit to finance. Judah had surveyed the Sacramento Valley and proposed a short-line railroad between bustling Sacramento and Joe Folsom's trading post about forty miles away. The trains could carry both passengers and freight to Folsom's end of the line and bring back ore on the return trip. It would tap most of the mother lode country, and if Judah's long-range plan succeeded this would be the first step in continuing over the Sierra Nevadas. The line should prove to be a financial bonanza.

It is unlikely that money was of much concern to Sam at that moment. His annual income was estimated at $250,000 to $500,000 per year, free of any taxes! His investments ranged from biscuit mills to bookstores, from lots to lumber mills. He lived lavishly, befitting his wealth. When Sam drank, everyone drank—often a thousand dollars' worth in a night. Sam scribbled IOUs on the backs of envelopes, and when necessary he initialed the corks of champagne bottles which his brother John, acting as bookkeeper honored the next day just as he would honor a bank draft. While others might settle for small rewards, Sam always went for broke.

Sam grabbed up Judah's scheme and ran with it. Dense throngs gathered on Washington's Birthday, 1856, to mark the dedication of the railroad between Sacramento and Folsom.

Sam was one of the principal speakers at the celebration, which was brief because everyone was anxious to ride the train. It was being pulled by the "C.K. Garrison," gaily draped with bunting. Mrs. Judah smashed a bottle of champagne over the panting engine, and it was officially placed in service. The engine chuffed out of the depot area and teakettled up the track. Brannan and William T. Sherman faced each other on the velour-covered seats in one of the three passenger cars which had been coupled together to carry a few of the dignitaries at the ceremony.

"This is a great day for California," Sam said with a broad smile.

"Hope it is a better day for investors," Sherman groused. "We should have also laid tracks to Marysville, I'm thinking."

"At sixty thousand dollars a mile?" Sam asked. "Maybe it'd be better to have this one pay off first."

"Don't believe it ever will," Sherman snapped. His estimate proved to be correct. The first railroad didn't pay, but it became in time the first link of the Central Pacific, the great transcontinental railroad that eventually spanned the nation.

But Sam's glancing interests couldn't be contained in a mere railroad. Significant events were taking place in San Francisco. Crime was rampant again and a second Vigilance Committee was being formed to put it down. Sam hurried back to the city to take part.

16 City of Turmoil

San Francisco was shedding its outer shell as a brawling, gold-mad city rampant with violence, but the infection of vice still remained. It had become a Sodom-by-the-Sea with a thin new veneer, where politicians attended such genteel diversions as lectures by Sarah Pellett, the women's suffrage advocate. Unfortunately too often her remarks were drowned out by the sounds of street brawls or gunfire. In the same issue, the *Alta Californian* told of the "Judith" performance along with an account of a bull running loose in the street, followed by yapping, maddened curs. A spooked stallion was roped and shot during the melee.

In spite of its rowdy atmosphere, San Francisco boasted more newspapers (20) than London; more books published then the rest of the trans-Mississippi area; three libraries; twenty-four public grade schools.

Even Sam was continually astonished by the fantastic growth and laughed at the squatter who was trying to stake his claim in Union Square at gun point. The squatters eventually organized to confound the city. San Franciscans didn't even wince when "Honest Harry" Meiggs, a favorite son, looted the city treasury of a fortune and everything else that wasn't bolted down, then skipped off to South America.

Such shenanigans could be accommodated in San Francisco's public conscience, but the breaking point was finally reached when a suave, slick-fingered New Orleans gambler named Charles Cora shot U. S. Marshal William Richardson one November day in 1855. The men fought over some alleged remarks made about Cora's paramour, Belle, queen of the Waverly Place demimonde. After a spirited discussion at the Blue Wing Saloon, Cora and Richardson left together, seemingly on good terms. Moments later a scuffle was followed by a shot. Richardson was mortally wounded and Cora walked away.

"What's been done?" Sam asked his friends once he was back in town. "Why hasn't Cora been punished?"

That vital question was being considered by others, many of whom had already signed the great register of a new Committee of Vigilance. The answer came in the doleful tolling of the Monumental fire bell. Two strikes, pause, two strikes, pause.

Sam was among the first to reach the Sacramento Street headquarters, but no one seemed certain as to what should be done. Sam talked with a few of his cronies. Then, as the throng enlarged, he stepped up on a bench. He pulled off his plug hat, opened his coat and jammed his hands in his pockets, assuming a cocky, defiant air.

"Shame on you men! Shame on San Francisco!" Sam said, sneering as he talked. "Has our great city become so morally flabby and so slothful that we'll now allow a common gambler to kill a United States marshal and do nothing about it?

"Have we no pride? No honor? No dignity? Doesn't anyone remember what happened before? Doesn't anyone remember what San Francisco was before we banded together to clean it up? The killings, the robberies, the arson? Are we going to tolerate crime again?"

Sam's voice rose as the crowd thickened. Several hundred had gathered to hear him, and the men were becoming restless, shuffling and obviously ready for action. Mutterings grew in volume, like the rumblings of a coming avalanche.

"What'll we do, Brannan? Take Cora from jail?"

Before Sam could answer, a squad of men pushed their way through the mob and grabbed Sam, dragging him from his bench. They were sheriff's deputies. Sam was told he was being arrested for inciting a riot and disturbing the peace. The deputies formed a flying wedge around Sam to keep the mob from grabbing him from their custody. Moving swiftly, they had Sam out of the mob before the roar of dismay could turn into action.

"Grab Brannan. Get those policemen!"

The officers brandished their weapons and continued walking, increasing their pace. Before the mob could organize Sam was inside police headquarters. Some of the throng followed the officers and gathered outside the police station.

Confident of his position, Sam refused to answer any questions. "You see those people outside? If you hold me long, there will be more and they'll come in and get me out. You heard the fire bell. You know the Vigilantes are going to regroup, and they'll take care of Cora no matter what the law decides. You'll save time by letting me go."

The officers consulted among themselves, occasionally glancing at Sam. Finally they told him to go; all charges were being dismissed.

Cora had been remanded to the care of Billy Mulligan, the sheriff. Sam suspected there would be trouble because he had done his street-corner best to rouse the people. He'd wait until the Vigilantes sounded the alarm and then act.

Though Sam was glad to be back in San Francisco and to have the excitement and companionship of his cronies in gambling and drinking, he was down-deep lonely. His wife, the children and her mother had all gone to Europe. They had taken a château in Geneva and the children were being sent to the finest of Continental schools. To assure them ample funds, Sam had some choice property set aside from which they were to get all of the income. Though Sam never engaged in a venture he didn't think would win, he was realist enough to know that slips were made and that king-doms could be lost for want of a nail.

When his brother John counseled caution, Sam only laughed. "I may not cut a long swath in life but it'll be a wide one."

Sam took a hurried excursion to Europe much later to try and prevail upon Eliza to return home. When she refused, he indulged himself in buying brood stock of fine Grampian sheep, prize cattle from England, and rare grape cuttings from all over Europe—all to be transplanted to California.

With his family away, Sam closed his Mission Street house and moved in with John and his family. He wanted people around, people who understood him as his brother did. Though he was at loose ends with himself, Sam helped or-ganize the E Clampus Vitus Society, which was put together "just for the fun of it" and lived up to its name for those pioneers who were invited to join.

At last the magnificent fire engine, which had cost Sam $10,000, arrived aboard the *Bostonian* after 103 days at sea. It was Sam's gift to the Howard Fire Company. Sam had ordered the engine three years before and it had been all this time in the making. It was worth the time and the money, however. Such an engine would make the Howard Company the best in San Francisco, and the celebration of acceptance of the gift was strictly a white-glove, red-shirt and brass-button affair.

The *Alta Californian* was apparently as pleased with the gift as Sam. ". . . The engine is one of the most complete and beautiful pieces of mechanism we have ever seen. Every portion of the steel and iron work is highly and heavily plated with silver . . . scroll work is graceful in design and perfect in finish . . . the woodwork is of the finest mahogany and

is enscribed with a griffin's head finely carved and gilded . . .
on the left side of the box is a landscape painting with horses,
trees and a lake with a boating party . . ."

Sam had all the basic instincts of a flamboyant showman,
and he delighted in displaying the new vehicle against the
backdrop of a city-wide celebration and parade. City officials
were there, as were marching units from all of the other
volunteer fire companies in San Francisco.

To everyone's dismay, the fine engine's reputation was
diminished by a rather inglorious occurrence not long afterward. While in performance of its duties, the engine's brakes
gave way on one of San Francisco's most precipitous hills, and
while the crew watched, horror-stricken, the machine went
rocketing down the incline, its bell clanging like all red fury.
It gathered such momentum that by the time it reached the
earthen embankment at Lombard Street it easily mounted
the slope without slowing and flung itself into a heap at the
bottom on the far side.

Sorrowfully, Sam dug down and paid for the extensive re-
pairs which were required to put his pet project back into
service.

Sam was enraged when he read that Cora's trial had re-
sulted in a hung jury and that the gambler had been returned to jail to await a new trial. Sam was determined to
start a clean-up campaign on his own again, but his brother
John advised against it. William T. Coleman, who had played
a modest and moderate part in the first Vigilance Committee,
was in full charge of the Second Committee and appeared
capable of handling the crimes in an orderly fashion. Sam
had showed the way once and realized that they had no real
need for him in the present affair.

Sam hated to miss the excitement, but he took no active
part in the Second Vigilance Committee, which lived up to
its purpose and promises. Shortly after Cora was returned
to jail to await a second trial, James Casey, an ex-convict and
ballot-box stuffer, murdered the militant newspaper editor

James King. With that outrage heaped on the smoldering public conscience, the Committee moved swiftly and hanged both Cora and Casey on the day of the editor's funeral.

After dispensing other summary justice for lesser criminals, the Committee again disbanded and held a final parade in August of 1856 in which Sam was an esteemed participant. Sam felt a warm glow at the honors accorded him and the fact that they remembered his earlier work.

With that chapter closed, Sam turned his interest again to the building of San Francisco. With Volney Howard, Sam Hensley and Eli Cook, he formed a syndicate to launch an efficient banking service in California.

Sam was able to raise money, and his proven ability attracted the others into the plan. But one man, Tom King, brother of the murdered editor, for some obscure reason disliked Sam and questioned his motives. Since the success of the bank would hinge on the stability of Sam Brannan, King was openly critical; but King was finally mollified when Sam showed up with a firm line of credit from the New York bankers, a group never known to take chances. Sam had put up $500,000 in property as collateral for the loans.

Some of the joy of the new venture, which was begun officially October 21, 1857, vanished when Sam's best friend Bill Howard died suddenly. It was a grievous loss of a staunch friend just as Sam was proudly opening the door of the new bank at the corner of Montgomery and California Streets.

Sam's bank did so well that he came up with a new twist which shocked the conservative financial circles, along with the irascible editor of the *Herald*. But Sam frequently proceeded on the premise if a little was good, more was better.

For a variety of reasons, currency became in short supply in California; to relieve the situation, Sam hit upon a plan which would help California a little and Sam a lot. He decided to issue his own currency. It was a bold imaginative step, worthy of Sam's predilection to solve problems according to his own lights.

King's *Evening Bulletin* took umbrage at the audacious
move in its November 16, 1857, issue. Their comment was
prompted when King dined in one of San Francisco's finest
restaurants and was able to pay for the meal in Brannan's
money. The new bills were not only accepted without question but U.S. legal tender was returned as change for the bill.

Sam's money was printed with the likeness of Washington
and Franklin, a railroad and a mining scene (which *The Herald* insisted cuttingly was Mormon Island) . ". . . Mr. Brannan violates the constitution with his pernicious 'shin plaster'
currency," it denounced in a scathing editorial, "and such
a move has been the policy of rotten banking institutions
who have brought ruin, distress and despair by flooding the
country with inflated paper money . . . Space will not permit us to allude to the tides of evil which will follow if Mr.
Brannan's scheme is tolerated. Let the danger be nipped in
the bud and the district attorney should prosecute the man
who boldly, in clear defiance of the laws, thrusts upon us a
miserable currency . . ."

Sam only laughed at John's insistence that he file a suit
for libel, but one citizen did file a complaint against the
public circulation of the currency. The charges came to nothing. "It doesn't matter much what they say, as long as my
name is spelled correctly," Sam smiled. "I'd rather have
King's spleen than his praise anyway."

Though the bank continued to succeed and prosper, Sam
gradually lost interest in it. His pursuits were always visionary projects which, once completed, no longer held his interest. Intolerant of tedium in any form, his interests bounced
here and there like a squirrel running on a willow branch.
Because Sam believed that the next day was more important
than the decades past, he became an angel for all sorts of
schemes, even some which were palpable frauds. He offered
a prize and guarantee of publication for anyone who would
write an acceptable epic poem about California. *Poetry of*

the Pacific, edited by May Wentworth, was published by H. H. Bancroft a few years after the offer appeared.

Sam had long neglected his land in Napa Valley and decided to do something about it. He savored the mineral water which flowed from artesian wells and could envision baths, healthful waters to drink—a spa to equal those anywhere in the world.

Soon his soaring imagination made this project the capstone for his empire, a place where he could rest without care. He would have a railroad linking it with the rest of the world. His blooded sheep and cattle would have free range; there would be a distillery to process the grapes which he would plant. Maybe even his own family would return to enjoy it with him. He thought of the latter rather wistfully, knowing full well that the schism between him and his wife was real and deep. His trip to Europe had been to prevail upon her to return. But he was coldly rebuffed. Perhaps later, she said. Perhaps, indeed, Sam snorted.

Because much of his San Francisco property was obligated for loans or for his family's income, Sam found himself short of enough money to develop the Napa Valley land as he desired. He began to sell sections of it to finance and promote the rest. The sales attracted other residents, and his property decreased again and again until he had the necessary working capital.

Like the djinn of lore, Sam pointed his finger and a mammoth hotel began to grow, streets appeared, thirty houses were erected to accommodate those who couldn't pay the hotel rates, a roller rink was built, stables were erected and filled with fine horses, an enormous reservoir was dug to provide water for the lush gardens and to pipe spring water into every hotel room. There was no end to Sam's expanding imagination.

This was to be Calistoga, where the Caliph of California would preside.

Sam's brother groaned and protested at such wild spending, and friends warned that there might be bleak days ahead because of a leveling off in California's gold-rush economy. "Doom criers. Hand-wringers," Sam scoffed. "Where is your imagination and faith in California?"

Sam didn't overlook a detail. He also believed that Calistoga could become the silk center of the world and imported not only silk worms but a forest of mulberry trees upon which they were to feed. Then a corporal's guard of Japanese gardeners was imported to oversee the entire operation.

The surrounding acres were tilled and planted with the finest wine grape cuttings; a wine press was installed, then a distillery was erected. Sam hired Lewis Keseberg, the tragic figure of the Donner Party who had been accused of cannibalism, to manage the distillery. It was a cruel irony that a man whose name was so closely linked with tragedy, death and misfortune would be involved in the distillery which, many claimed, helped begin the dissolution of the Brannan empire.

Sam's physician warned that he should rest, take a voyage perhaps, and relieve himself of the burden he was carrying. "When I develop Calistoga the way I dream, then I will retire and rest," Sam answered. "I'll have all the money I will ever need and a place to enjoy myself. I am over forty now but still have much zip. You can't just turn that off."

John shook his head at Sam's gigantic spending but on orders he sold the Marysville properties and mortgaged others. It took a lot of money to build the enormous hotel with its annex and to establish a stage line to bring the expected guests. Sam also established a cemetery in which he planned to have all of his family buried. Curiously, he provided space for everyone except himself. But this was typical—he didn't ever really expect to die.

His son Don Francisco was reburied there. It was a day of sad memories for Sam, who spent most of the day on Mount

Lincoln, a high knoll which overlooked much of his Calistoga domain.

Three years after Sam began his planning, Calistoga officially opened. It was a memorable event. Everything was free. Food, drink and accommodations were provided for hundreds who responded to the engraved invitations. Sam chartered coaches to bring the guests, and they were served food and drink enroute. Favors of jewelry were given to both men and women, and a grand ball climaxed the opening celebrations. But what had begun as an elegant evening almost ended in tragedy when the hilarity was interrupted with the whooping of Indians.

Clad in loin cloths, paint and little else, the Indians leaped and danced among the elegantly clad guests, brandishing weapons and shrieking war whoops. For a moment all was wild confusion as women screamed, some fainted and men dashed about helplessly. Then the threat was over, when the Indians, as though by some common signal, headed whooping for the swimming pools where they dove into the water and began frolicking and splashing in the mud baths.

"That's Sam Brannan for you!" one guest cried. "He got those Indians filled up on brandy, then purposely turned them loose on the ballroom just to liven up the party a little!"

He was right. Sam was going to see to it that no one ever forgot the grand opening of Calistoga, and there were not a few who noted that before the evening was over Sam was every bit as drunk as his Indians.

17 Brannan's Battalion

John had cautioned his brother that Calistoga might become an unbearable financial strain and he agreed with Sam that a trip to New York must be made to acquire more capital. Sam had spared no expense in providing the finest possible accommodations for those who would come to his spa and leave their ailments, along with some money. But the costs were tremendous and he had to get help.

Money was tight now because of the Civil War but Brannan's reputation was sufficient to raise the necessary capital again. He celebrated his success with some New York financiers at the St. Nicholas Hotel, spending most of his time at the bar.

"Drinks for the house," a strange bull-horn voice called. "The drinks are on Cap'n Farnham."

Slowly Sam lowered his drink and swung toward the man who had made the announcement. He was an outsized man, handsome, his face deeply tanned, and was dressed in the blue uniform of a ship's officer.

"Are you the captain of the *Wanderer?*" Sam asked in a quiet tone.

The man nodded, then snarled: "What's it to you?"

"I don't drink with any such slaving scum as you," Sam said, his voice cutting with sarcasm. "I won't even breathe the same air. You pollute it, and I am leaving if you stay."

A silence suddenly draped over the men at the bar. Sam's slurs would have been an open invitation to trouble, a blood-letting, at any time, but they were particularly provocative when the men's passions were covered over by the thinnest veneer during wartime. Farnham was a notorious slaver and had been jailed in Savannah but had been released through a violent jail delivery launched by Southern sympathizers.

Farnham strode toward Sam and as he reached him began throwing punches. Sam ducked and rolled with the blows. The others milled about in the saloon and someone drew a pistol. A shot was fired. Men rushed for the bat-wing doors, but as they were pushing out, night patrolmen crashed in from the street. Swinging billy clubs, a few thuds, groans and falling bodies, and the melee was over. Sam was arrested, but Captain Farnham had somehow managed to disappear.

At precinct headquarters, Sam came up with $500 in coin to post a peace bond and was promptly released, but thanks to the wondrous new Pony Express service, his escapade was printed in the October 16, 1860, issue of the *Alta Californian,* only twenty-one days after the event. It was one time Sam didn't appreciate progress. Ann Eliza had just about decided to return to San Francisco but quickly changed her mind when she read of her husband's latest spree. She wrote indignantly that she didn't care for returning to a country where men, especially her own husband, didn't know how to behave themselves in public. Despite her refusal to join him, Sam returned to California happy and optimistic about the future, but unhappiness was waiting.

John's health had deteriorated rapidly following a siege of pneumonia and his doctor had suggested a sea voyage to restore his strength. But John wasn't equal to it. His lung fever, as advanced pneumonia was then called, killed him while at sea. His body was brought back carefully preserved in a cask of samshu, a potent Chinese liquor.

Sam wept openly at the funeral rites for his brother and, when he returned to his office, made arrangements for perpetual care for John's wife and family.

He missed John's good judgment in guiding his affairs as he continued with the development and expansion of the Calistoga property, including the construction of a short-line railroad. Sam had planned the railroad to connect Calistoga with the rest of the world, starting at Sacramento. To aid his cause, he became a lobbyist and established headquarters in the state capitol to entertain and influence legislators, spending thousands of dollars in the process. Senators and assemblymen were brought free to the Calistoga hotel and given the "cure."

But Sam apparently spent his money well. The Napa Valley railroad emerged from the bouquet of the champagne bottle and the smoke of fine Havana cigars which Sam provided for one and all. The railroad was chartered by the state and the subsidies necessary for the construction were to be provided by the local political divisions.

Obediently, Napa County supervisors voted subsidies which ranged from $5,000 to $10,000 per mile, and Sam's railroad began to take shape. Thousands of pigtailed coolies swarmed into the area. They had an interpreter to goad them into more work, and usually an Irish track boss was put in charge of overall operations.

Sam's intrusion into the field of California railroading, first in the Sacramento Valley and now in Napa, was considered an open threat and challenge by Mark Hopkins, Charles Crocker, Leland Stanford and Henry Huntington, four powerful Sacramento merchants who were now promoting the Central Pacific Railroad, the western end of the proposed transcontinental railroad. Considering California railroading their private domain, they looked with disfavor on such upstarts as Sam.

With Judah, Sam had been at the start of the trackage which would be the western terminal of the transcontinental railroad, and he still held a hefty share of the stock. The Big Four, as the four merchants were called, applied financial pressure by buying up Sam's debts, then demanding immediate payment. But Sam was able to come up with the necessary money. He refused to sell his stock, and he refused to be pushed out. Stubbornly he raised loan after loan to stave off the crushing pressure, but the task was almost too much for him. He needed another manager and he turned to Alex Badlam, Jr., the nephew of whom he had always been so fond. It proved to be an excellent choice.

Together they managed a financial coup which strengthened Sam's position. Through agents, Sam gradually sold all of his stock but took back shares in the Central Pacific, along with some cash. Now he had a foothold within the Big Four's domain, and whenever they prospered, so did Sam. Besides that, the stock made a fine collateral on which he could now borrow money to stave off the Big Four's pressures.

With this new cash, Sam bought more acreage around his Calistoga resort area, bringing it to more than two thousand acres, even though he had sold some to revive his flagging resources. Calistoga was rapidly becoming the "in" place for society figures. Even the great P. T. Barnum paid a visit, and Sam, who did not like to be outshone by anyone, determined to prove to Barnum he was a showman too.

After prior arrangement with a waiter, Sam led Barnum to one of the mineral springs which flowed through six-inch pipes. Standing by the mouth, the waiter held a plate on which there were two steaming fish. When Sam approached, the waiter reported sadly that the fishing hadn't been good that day, and the two steaming fish were all that he had been able to catch. Solemnly, Sam ordered them prepared for Mr. Barnum's dinner.

Walking on, Sam pointed out another "hot soup" spring. Here a table was set with crackers, soup plates and silverware.

Sam ladled up some of the hot liquid and Barnum tasted it. To his astonishment he found it did taste like soup, and he saw that there were even vegetables and meat in the liquid. By prearrangement Sam had a waiter slip in bits of solid matter as needed for the demonstration.

"Sam, you can have a job with me anytime," Barnum said. "You have the flair for showmanship and legerdemain. Imagine taking all this time and trouble to hoax your guests. Delightful."

Sam's Napa Valley estate was virtually an empire in itself and he was landlord to most of Calistoga. In addition to the flourishing commercial and residential properties, he ran hundreds of head of blooded cattle, horses and merino sheep on the grazing lands which surrounded the spa. Generally, Sam was on good term with the neighboring farmers, and many of them replanted their fields in wine grapes, which found a ready market at his distillery where his wine presses used nearly 3,000 tons of grapes to produce 100,000 gallons of brandy a year.

But difficulty arose because the farmers were dependent on the streams which flowed from the slopes of Mt. St. Helena and adjacent hills. They complained that Sam's stock, especially the sheep, roiled and fouled their drinking water. Obligingly, Sam hired additional shepherds to oversee the flocks and keep them from the water, but the trouble simmered and the farmers still complained. Sam's patience, at best, had a very low threshold and he felt he was being put upon with the continued haranguing. "You simply don't like the people who spend money at the resort. You're petty, mean and cheap," Sam snapped to the next complainers.

When one of his shepherds died, Sam believed he had been murdered, though others insisted his death was the result of a fall.

The feud smoldered, its fires near the surface. Open warfare seemed inevitable when some night-riders using dogs herded scores of Sam's sheep to a precipice and mercilessly drove them over the cliff to their deaths.

Alex talked Sam out of strapping on a gun and looking for the people involved. Instead, he persuaded Sam to file a complaint with the police, but they took little interest in the matter, believing that Sam was strong enough to police his own properties.

"And that's exactly what'll be done if there's a next time," Sam shouted in anger. "If I catch any others trespassing on my land, they'll get their answer from a gun. And you can tell everyone just that."

Over the years Brannan had spurned most public office. In 1853 when his name was placed on the ballot as candidate for the California assembly, he refused to make a speech or help his backers in any way. Despite this he was swept into office in a landslide, and his only public act as assemblyman was to renounce the office. But he had been on the city council and now, because of the Civil War and Lincoln's espousal of the anti-slavery issue, poured both money and energy into Lincoln's campaign. In tandem with Bill Ralston, head of the powerful Bank of California, Sam spearheaded a Lincoln campaign when the Republican Convention was held in Platt's Hall, San Francisco, on June 9, 1864.

Sam was the principal speaker and he showed that he had lost none of the crowd-pleasing magic. He had the zeal of a reformer and his anti-slavery spark caught the mood of the crowd. Flags were waved, drums banged and men shouted until they were hoarse. Even the most genteel of ladies waved their lace handkerchiefs in approval of Sam's fervent appeal for Lincoln. The hall shook with stamping feet and the thunder of the band playing, "We Are Coming, Father Abraham."

The electors showed their appreciation by naming Sam Brannan as one of the presidential electors, his name appearing with J. C. McCallum, Charles Maclay, William W. Crane and Warner Oliver.

Sam returned to his Montgomery Street offices following the convention. It was now the center of a great empire: the four-story Masonic Hall, a quarter-million-dollar Wells

Fargo Express office, the Armory for the California Light Guard, his bank, to say nothing of the 200 acres in west San Francisco. Despite all this opulence, Sam never seemed to get further ahead of his obligations than the next day. But he never flinched from either his obligations or the opportunity to take another chance, and what seemed like a fantastic opportunity appeared as he sat in his office one day.

Two men came in and introduced themselves as representatives of the Mexican government. One was General Gaspar Ochoa, the other, Placida Vargas. They had been advised that "Señor del Brannan" was a man always interested in making sound investments and advancing the causes of oppressed people. Sam, his interest already piqued, asked them to be seated.

During the Civil War, Napoleon III had believed it a propitious time to establish an empire in Mexico, as his first foothold in the western hemisphere. Accordingly, with the support of French troops, Maximilian, an Austrian archduke, had been persuaded to accept the crown and was sent to Mexico during 1864. But he soon found the Mexicans hostile to him and loyal to Benito Juarez, their Indian leader, whose headquarters were located at El Paso del Norte. (Ultimately, French support was withdrawn by Napoleon, the paper empire crumbled away and Maximilian was executed by a firing squad.)

"We are here to sell bonds to help finance the war against Maximilian and the French," the men said. "We need money, we need men and we need food."

Sam was only vaguely aware of the plight of the insurgents, but he was sympathetic with the people struggling for freedom and with Juarez, who was trying to lead the ragged masses. Only one thing bothered him. This was another filibuster. He had led the Mormons into California hoping to seize the land for a colony, and he had tried to usurp the Hawaiian Islands. These had been notable failures, but the spirit of adventure and expansion was in the air. He didn't fancy the prospect of France taking over Mexico. Yes, he would help.

The Mexicans explained that they would sell their bonds for about 10 percent of their face value—not because the bonds wouldn't be honored but simply because of the risk involved.

"All right, I'll take a million dollars' worth," Sam said explosively. The Mexicans beamed. Then Sam said: "No, I'll take one and a half million. That'll cost me a hundred and fifty thousand." Sam didn't know where the money was coming from, but he never doubted he could raise it.

The Mexicans were overjoyed with his offer. It was more than they had any right to dream of. "You'll never regret it, Señor del Brannan," the General said. "We will never forget an act of such generosity. We are forever in your debt."

Though considerably poorer, Sam felt good inside.

Alex didn't feel good though when Sam told him of the commitment and ordered some property sold to raise the necessary money. "Have you lost your mind?" Alex asked angrily. "Don't you realize there is a limit to your resources and generosity? That you are already skirting the edge of disaster?"

Sam was adamant and the bonds were purchased as agreed. He even arranged to get more money for additional assistance. Another $50,000 was raised for what came to be known as "Brannan's Battalion."

With the gold veins showing signs of anemia, times in California were somewhat chancy and uncertain. Men were unemployed and others were dissatisfied with the return they had received from the diggings. They were eager for something new. Sam realized these men were ripe for service in a fighting unit to help Juarez. While it was illegal to raise an army within the United States for any sort of military adventures, the news of the possible excursion to Mexico was passed in whispers.

Even Sam's enthusiasm didn't anticipate the response he

received to his recruitment campaign. He tried to accommodate every volunteer and carefully selected the leaders. Once the Battalion was organized, small groups were infiltrated into Mexico so their numbers would not be noticed. Weapons were also sent in small shipments under the guise of farm implements, books or other harmless cargoes to various Mexican ports, then forwarded to men in the back country. While Brannan's Battalion was but a tiny fraction of the men already fighting under Juarez, they did bring skill, weapons and, best of all, the Yankee dollar to pump up the spirit and the economy of the struggling nation. The mere appearance of foreign troops would reveal to Maximilian that the United States was covertly sending men and supplies, for the presence of the foreign intruder was against the Monroe Doctrine and had been publicly branded as an outrage. While Brannan's Battalion would never be credited with any significant military victory, Sam's personal, unflinching support with money, men and supplies had a tremendous effect in bringing about ultimate victory.

Sam's motive had never been predicated upon a return on his investment. Secretly, he was even surprised when he received the engraved bonds in an alligator leather packet. He would have given the money just as quickly without assurances of return. Realistically, Sam knew that even if Juarez were successful in establishing a stable government, it would be a long, long time before the government was financially sound enough to repay foreign debts.

The Civil War had cast a pall over the nation, but Sam still hadn't lost his exuberance. When news was received that Charleston had been taken by the Union Army, he considered it an event worthy of celebration. He prepared a full stand-up banquet for hundreds of his San Francisco pals. Three buildings were illuminated from roof to cellar, and every window was draped with bunting and flags. Employees fetched wood for huge bonfires to be touched off at the intersection of California and Sacramento Streets.

Coat off, his brocaded vest hanging open, Sam warmly greeted all of his guests, speaking to them over the din of laughter, talking, Roman candles and the Chinese bombs. But for Sam that wasn't enough. He sent some employees to confiscate Bluxome's old signal cannon and it was wheeled into place and touched off. There was a gigantic roar.

"That's the ticket," Sam hollered. "Touch it off again!"

In all, it was fired thirty-six times in honor of each of the United States.

But even before the last salute had been fired, complaints were pouring in. Windows everywhere were being broken by the cannon's roar. "Forget it!" Sam ordered. "Keep up the celebration. Tell them to send me their bills!"

Later it cost Sam $2500 just to replace all of the broken panes, but this was only one cost of the huge celebration. It was a minor discomfort compared to the news that word of Charleston's capture was premature. The city hadn't been taken; there had been no reason for the celebration at all.

For some time after it was dangerous to even mention the word "Charleston" in Sam's presence; but eventually, as in all other things, he began to see the humorous side and laugh at himself.

"I guess the joke's on me," he admitted. "Damn the cost, we had a lot of fun, didn't we?"

18 The Empire

Sam was elated with the news that his wife and family were finally returning to San Francisco, after being in Europe for such a long time. It had taken another trip by Sam and the firm promise of good conduct to get her to relent and come back. Even though Sam had houses in San Francisco, Sacramento and a vast estate in southern California near Los Angeles, he felt that he should get her something extra special.

Because Sam had no one else, he had been living alone at the Russ House, one of San Francisco's best hotels. Until he could get his family permanently settled, he arranged for an enormous suite of rooms to accommodate them. "My family." How sweetly those words rolled on his tongue. He had almost despaired of ever having them back again.

With Alex, Sam drove over most of San Francisco trying to decide which mansion would best suit Ann Eliza and the children. He finally selected a fine house on Clay Street which was perched high on a hill and had a sweeping view of both the city and the Bay. The house, replete with gingerbread frescoes, contained dozens of rooms as well as a carriage house and a stable. Unfurnished, high-ceilinged and gloomy with its dark paneling, it depressed Sam, but he realized there was one way to lighten it.

"We'll get a wagon load of furniture and pile it here for Ann Eliza to choose from," Sam said.

Alex shook his head. "No, Sam, that won't do. You know how she is. She'll want it her way, and no other. There's no use wasting a lot of money buying things she won't use."

Sam nodded sadly. He had first fallen in love with Ann Eliza because of her haughty ways, but he did feel that her manner had grown increasingly imperious and unnecessarily chill when she was around him. Well, maybe things would be different after this long separation, he hoped.

The reunion did not bode well when Ann Eliza allowed Sam no more than a peck on the cheek when they arrived by ship. More disappointing, all of the children proved equally stand-offish, treating Sam like a stranger instead of their father.

His son was a young man now and claimed to be an engineer. The girls curtsied to their father and extended cool fingertips as they would to a stranger. Sam ran his own finger around the inside of his collar and felt choked up and uncomfortable.

He continued to feel like an outsider even after they had furnished and moved into the Clay Street residence. He was aghast at the staff of servants, maids, coachmen and cooks which his wife said were necessary. When he pointed to the cost, she replied that he simply didn't understand how people of culture lived.

The Clay Street house immediately became the mecca for the bohemian set of San Francisco—the poets, painters and poseurs. Sam's objections to paying the bills to these spongers were met with sniffs from Ann Eliza, who said it was a man's place to support his wife and reminded him that she could always return to Europe. His daughters signed bills throughout San Francisco's finest shops, and young Sam bought whatever took his fancy with the statement: "See my father, Sam Brannan. He's good for it."

Brannan had became increasingly disenchanted with his son, who traded on the fact that he was a qualified mining engineer. When Sam inquired when he was going to apply his knowledge and get a job, the young man said that he hadn't been able to find work anywhere.

"Did you expect to find it in a gambling hall or a saloon?" Sam asked icily. "You are over twenty-one. It's time you get some dirt on your hands."

His son reddened and excused himself from the dinner table.

When he had gone, Ann Eliza said sharply, "Don't you pick on that boy, Sam. You are a fine one to say anything about drinking or gambling considering the example you've set for him!"

"Ann Eliza Corwin Brannan," Sam said in an ominous tone. "I've never denied you one thing, but if you think your European manners are too hoity-toity for a roughneck like me, remember I paid for your being able to learn 'em. I know your airs are too much for me, and things are going to change. That is my final word on the subject." Sam slammed down his napkin and left the table. "Well, I never!" he heard his wife's disapproving comment.

Soon after this, Sam reopened his Montgomery Street apartment and began spending most of his time either there or in Calistoga, instructing Alex Badlam to pay all of the family bills without any question.

Though Sam's dream of his family making their home at the Calistoga resort had been shattered, he was determined to find something they would like. He went to Los Angeles and bought the Abel Stearns property, believing it would make a wintering place for them because of the balmy climate. But Ann Eliza rebuffed the gift coldly and didn't even bother to visit it.

With that lash across the open wound of his already raw

temperament, Sam was in a violent mood by the time he returned to Calistoga and almost welcomed the trouble which awaited him.

A couple of years previously, he had leased a parcel of land to a man named Warner Buck. There was a small, steam-operated sawmill and a pumping plant on the property, but Buck had defaulted on his rent agreement and Sam demanded that he either pay up the back rent or relinquish the property. Buck was a leading member in the "Hate Brannan" club which still flourished in the Napa Valley and ignored Brannan's demands. When Sam applied legal pressure to recover the rent or his property, Buck declared himself bankrupt and arranged to transfer his lease to friends, Andy Snyder and Milton McDowell.

Convinced that he had been cheated, Sam sent a notice to Buck, Snyder and McDowell to vacate the property immediately. They sent a defiant refusal. Sam strode to the Calistoga hardware store, bought a pair of guns to swing on each hip and headed for the sawmill. Two of Sam's friends, Swift and Garret, tried to dissuade him from overt action.

"Those men will be armed too and expecting you," Swift warned.

"I don't give a damn if they are," Sam replied angrily. "I've been cheated and I mean to set it right."

Swift and Garret decided to accompany him when they were unable to talk Sam out of the attack. They had walked within shooting distance of the mill when they heard a shouted command:

"Halt! You men stay where you are or there'll be trouble."

Sam hesitated, trying to discover by sound just where the speaker was located, then slowly walked toward the mill.

"I formally demand that you give up unlawful possession of my property," Sam shouted as he continued to walk forward. "I mean to have my place, peaceably or not. I don't care which."

"Halt! Stop or we'll shoot. You are trespassing."

Sam muttered that the voice sounded like Snyder's, though he wasn't certain. His friends were grim, looking straight ahead watching, though neither was armed.

A shot thundered, followed closely by another. Then another shot . . . another.

Sam's expression seemed one of surprise, but for a few seconds his pace never slackened. At each shot his body jerked convulsively. Blood showed through on his clothes. His hands dropped toward his guns but came away empty as he finally pitched forward and lay still on the ground.

His companions rushed to his side. Swift gave a cursory look at Sam's wounds, then hollered to Garrett, "Go get a doctor, quick. I think he's dying. He's been hit bad."

Although it had sounded like only a few shots, five had been fired in all. And each one had hit its target. A physician from the Calistoga resort rushed to the scene, stanching Sam's blood as best he could.

"There's a bad one in the neck, just missed the jugular vein. Could've killed him right off. Might die anyway," the doctor said as he worked. There was another wound in the area above the hip, near a kidney. Sam was unconcious as the doctor loaded him aboard a buggy. "You'd better notify his kin as quickly as possible," he said.

"As bad as that?" his friends inquired.

The doctor nodded. "He may recover if there aren't any complications. He'll be lucky if he ever walks again."

Alex Badlam arrived in Calistoga immediately after he received the telegram telling of Sam's condition. He had urged Ann Eliza to accompany him but she refused, observing that it was probably the result of another of Sam's disgraceful brawls. She did not tell the chldren that their father had been shot.

Officers apprehended the men responsible and they were held in lieu of $5,000 bail. Sam was near death, but his constitution and will to live were strong. As he began to recover, he refused to press charges, and the men who had nearly killed him were released.

"Sam, those men tried to kill you," Alex said angrily. "If you had pressed charges that would have stopped all of the trouble you have been having here."

"No, I provoked them into the fight," Sam replied, as he shook the cane which he now needed to get around. "I asked for the fight, and if nothing else, I've learned something from it."

What Sam had established in his own mind was that his long marriage to Ann Eliza was finally at an end. He was bitter that she hadn't cared enough to come to him when he was near death. Though he had long suspected this day was coming, the finality of the truth still came as a surprise and a shock when he was served with divorce papers charging him with a variety of indiscretions.

"Odd that she didn't notice all those faults when I was paying her bills," Sam observed caustically as he handed over the papers to Alex. "Have our attorney look at these, then give her whatever she asks."

Alex, after consultation with the attorneys, approached Sam with a grim countenance. "She's asking for half of all your property and holdings, and she wants it in cash."

Alex's words were the thunderclap of doom for Sam's empire. His success had always hinged upon the dynamic economy, where he had to spend to make more and one property paid another. But once the cash was squeezed out of the empire, the obligations would become top-heavy and the whole house of cards would crumble. The knell was sounded on November 11, 1870, when the decree was entered in a San Francisco court under the jurisdiction of Judge Morrison. There, referees were appointed to preside over the dissolution of Sam Brannan's estate.

"Chalk one up for sin," Sam commented ruefully when he was allowed uncontested title to 45,000 gallons of Calistoga brandy valued at $100,000.

Ann Eliza had spurned the brandy because she didn't want money which was derived from such a sale, even though she had lived for years from the same distillery profits.

But she proved to be less haughty when it came to other readily convertible assets. She obtained title to eight city blocks in San Francisco, located not far from the Mission Delores and immensely valuable. She also got 200 shares in the Central Pacific railroad which Sam had contrived to retain despite the pressures of the Big Four; more than a thousand shares in Sam's banks, which alone were worth more than $150,000; and a number of other enormously valuable securities and properties.

The settlement ran into the hundreds of thousands of dollars, and the Brannans could rack up another California first. It was the largest divorce settlement made in California up to that time, and for many, many years to come.

"It's only money. I'll make another fortune," Sam boasted, but this time some of his old confidence was lacking. When he and Alex totted up the disaster, they both realized that he was ruined. Though he had been relieved of the crushing expenses of his wife and family, he no longer had the assets on which he could borrow money for his investments. For the time being, Sam decided to retire to Calistoga, but he never visualized it would be under these circumstances. The retirement was brief. Creditors trailed him and claimed the spa also, and the Central Pacific finally succeeded in taking even his Napa Valley railroad.

Sam's financial debacle left Alex Badlam without a job, and he turned to politics. Elected supervisor of San Francisco County, Alex continued to keep a lookout for Sam, since he was now over fifty and otherwise alone in the world. To anyone who would listen, Sam outlined his new attack on the world, but he dragged himself about with a cane and gave little sign of the courage needed for such an assault.

There were a few lots left in Napa Valley and Sam was

able to get options on others. He found an active market for the property, so much so that one attorney drew 300 deeds for him in a single year. With new cash available, Sam's spirits soared. He tried to keep up appearances by always being clean-shaven and dressing sprucely. He was whistling a bright tune when he received a note inviting him to dine with some of his old friends on July 31, 1876. There were some matters of importance to be discussed.

Sam arrived in San Francisco early that day and went to the barbershop where he had been a regular patron for many years. He ordered the full treatment of haircut, shave, facial, manicure and shine. But no one would take a cent for their services.

"No, Sam, this one is on us," they told him. "You have paid for it many times over."

Sam felt a warm glow that someone still remembered him and the old days as he walked away toward the Pioneer Building. There hung a large oil painting of Sam Brannan of the old days. Perhaps he could see it again. But then, Sam considered, who would remember Sam Brannan now?

He pushed through the swinging doors into the gloomy building. His head was down and he walked into a knot of people before he realized it. He looked up. Above them in huge letters on a long banner were the words:

WELCOME SAM BRANNAN. THE MAN WHO BUILT SAN FRANCISCO.

Some of the men rushed forward to grab his hand, others clapped him on the back. "What's this? What's this all about?" Sam asked confusedly.

Judge Hall cleared his thoat, then intoned in his best judicial manner, "Sam Brannan, it was thirty years ago this date, on July 31, 1846, that you first sailed through the Golden Gate into what was then Yerba Buena."

Sam's face creased into a huge smile. "Well, I'll be. That's right. Can it be that long, though?"

Just then the band thundered out with a stirring tune. "That's the 'Sam Brannan March' and was written especially for you," Judge Hall reminded.

The Society of California Pioneers, which Sam had organized so long ago, the Musical Fund Society and members of the old Howard Fire Company No. 3 had all cooperated in sponsoring the affair to honor Sam. Pioneer Hall was draped with flags and bunting, a fine banquet had been prepared and Professor Spandini had written special music in honor of the man whom the program described as San Francisco's First Citizen.

Judge Hall gave a long eloquent speech reciting some of Sam's accomplishments, recalling that he had led the first emigrants to California, preached the first sermon, performed the first marriage, been defendant in the first trial, founded the first San Francisco newspaper, become the City's first millionaire, along with a number of other significant firsts.

Others recalled his founding the Vigilantes, and McGiffen said: "Here, too, we have the real father of the great Central Pacific Railroad. Though Sam no longer owns it, it was his Sacramento railroad over which the first trains started, and it was the Sacramento terminal where the transcontinental trains first lit their boiler fires. Both California and San Francisco had much to thank Sam Brannan for."

Sam responded to all the glowing tributes with a short, modest speech, his voice choked with emotion. Later, after the long day of events and excitement, Sam got a chance to talk with Alex alone. He instructed his nephew to clean up his affairs and pay off everyone he owed, so long as the money lasted, explaining simply that he was moving on to make a new start. Sam believed that he hadn't lost the magic touch and he could make another fortune. Alex agreed sadly.

While the wreckage of the finances was being cleared away, Sam returned to the Napa Valley. He spent a great deal of time on Mt. Lincoln near Don Francisco's grave, thinking about the future and the past. When Alex informed him that things were in the best possible shape, and there was still enough left to provide a very modest income, Sam decided to move on. Sam didn't know that this income was being provided primarily out of Alex's pocket.

Sam believed that his San Francisco affairs were now closed. The book would open again much farther south. In Mexico, if things went the way he planned, he would launch a new quest for the golden, elusive fleece of fortune.

19 The Penultimate

While Sam Brannan was willing to admit that he had been stripped of his fortune, he didn't agree with those who thought he had also lost his wits.

His wife's attorneys had spurned the Mexican bonds with a par value of one and a half million dollars. But Sam had been glad to keep them, and they were tucked away in a satchel as he sailed out of San Francisco Bay bound for Monterey, a short distance down the California coast. If he could recover even what he had paid for them, $150,000, Sam knew that amount would make a rather secure starting block for another financial pyramid.

His agent, Manuel Castro, met him when he stepped ashore at Monterey. Castro had agreed to assist Señor Brannan on a contingent fee, that is, his fee would be determined by the amount collected, if anything. Castro was a prominent figure in Mexican and American affairs since the days when he had led the Mexican forces in California against the Americans during the Mexican War.

Together Castro and Sam contacted Mexican officials, but the only satisfaction they got was the suggestion that a trip to Mexico City might be most fruitful. Sam had the small amount of cash which Alex sent him and charitably called "rent money." Though it was far from his usual standard of travel, Sam didn't grumble at sailing steerage to the Mexican capital. He and Castro ate from a basket brought from Monterey until their food was exhausted, after which they were able to share with some of the other passengers.

Castro seized an opportunity to get a bigger share of the proceeds. "I don't think the Mexican government will deal with a Norte Americano," he said. "If the bonds are in my name, a Mexican, there would be a better chance that we'd get something. I'll do it for half the money."

At first, Sam angrily refused, saying that he believed the Mexicans would honor their obligation to him, if to anyone. But when he cooled down, he agreed to consider the offer. He might be a hard man to bluff but he was not a fool.

After arrival, they were shunted from one Mexican official to another, but finally reports began to filter back to San Francisco that Brannan had been allowed a large grant of land in exchange for the value of his bonds. In the issue of January 18, 1881, The Sacramento *Union* reported:

"Sam Brannan states that his claims have been allowed and that reports to the contrary are false. He is waiting at this writing for the final disposition to be made to Castro, an aide who is assisting him in presenting his claim . . ."

A shadow was thrown over Sam's successes in another, smaller story which appeared in the same issue of The *Union*. The correspondents told of a rebellion of the Yaqui Indians and the withdrawal of the Mexican troops who had been unable to cope with the fierce tribesmen. The story also related that a number of settlers in the area had been killed.

The scene of the uprising happened to be on the very land which had been granted Sam!

He appeared to have been swallowed up in Mexico, because it was more than a year before anyone heard from him. Then on February 18, 1882, Alex received a terse but jubilant telegram.

"GRANT FOR 1500 LEAGUES IN SONORA CON-
FIRMED IN ADDITION TO OTHER SMALLER
CLAIMS. AREA WILL COLONIZE ONE THOUSAND
FAMILIES."

In a letter which followed, Sam explained that Castro had
been put in charge of a military unit designed to protect the
settlers while the Yaqui Indians were being civilized. However, the Indians were reluctant to accept liberation such
as this, and the rebellion continued.

Sam was welcomed as a hero when he made a trip to New
York a short time later in an effort to obtain money for
financing the colonization of his new land grant. A provi-
sion of the grant was that he would populate the land. But
that required money and had prompted Sam to return to
the scene of previous conquests. He found adventurers who
were eager to begin a new life in Mexico:

"Señor del Brannan is the favorite Norte Americano and
son of Mexico," enthusiastic Mexicans said of him. He was
called a patriot and one who had held the light of hope
when Mexico writhed under the rule of Maximilian. Now
he could live as grandee on the land of Mexico.

At a banquet honoring Sam, the honorable Dwight Town-
send spoke in behalf of the United States, tendering the hand
of friendship to the southern neighbors. Ed Kemble, Sam's
former employee and now a member of the Associated Press,
recalled Sam's long and illustrious career in the building of
San Francisco, and in all it was another glorious day in Sam's
life.

But for all his past deeds, the old magic seemed gone. Following his New York tour, which proved to be a failure in
raising money, Sam returned to San Francisco hoping that
he would be able to raise the money there. Such funds as
he obtained he immediately used to pay surveyors to plot the
cities and farms which he planned. With his funds running
low, Sam offered to match acreages with anyone buying a
lot in the promised land.

"For each lot you buy, I'll deed one free," he advertised. "And that offer stands, even if you buy a farm. You'll have another one free of all charges."

San Francisco hadn't forgotten its wandering son. Sam was the guest of honor at the Palace Hotel, and once again at the Pioneer Hall. His speeches were faithfully reported in the San Francisco newspapers, but buyers were slim and extremely reluctant about investing in this property they had never seen. Even the old slogan "Sam Brannan buys it" or "Sam Brannan endorses it" failed to open the pocketbooks as it had previously. He was puzzled as to why his friends couldn't see the advantage of his land promotion.

"They've lost their sense of adventure. No one has any imagination anymore," Sam complained.

Because Sam had sent what cash he raised to his surveyors and used the rest in promotional schemes, he had to obtain an advance from Alex to pay his return passage to Mexico.

Some San Franciscans wondered if their conservatism was justified when they read of Sam's being granted $10,000 against future income, to finance more engineering and surveying charges. Also, his grant of land was relocated to a more hospitable area, out of the rebellious Indian territory. To many, including Sam, it appeared that his staunchness had been rewarded.

But Fortune turned her face the other way. Sam had used up too much time. He was officially dispossessed from his land because of not making required improvements within a specified period, and the Mexican lands were forfeited.

Sam was stunned with the change of fortunes, and for a long time he wrote no one. He found solace in drinking and his ambition seeped away. In a foreign land without friends or money, he realized how Captain John Sutter must have felt when he had watched his empire crumble and slip away without being able to do anything. It was maddening, but Sam had no one even to vent his anger upon. Alex, as usual, was the only one who came to his aid and sent him money enough to keep going.

During a low ebb, Sam met John Ricketson, an American who had chosen Mexico to spend his leisurely days. Ricketson, who had become almost a native, indulged in real estate sales and was immediately interested when Sam told him of the land grant. Ricketson helped Sam prepare another application for a grant of land and was astounded when the appeal was granted by the Mexican government.

Immediately, Brannan and Ricketson planned a horseback tour of the land to prepare for exploitation. It was such an immense grant that it took them fifty days just to ride around it. The grant included about two million acres. Even Ricketson, who was by nature more conservative than Sam, became enthusiastic over the prospect of what could be done with the land. They returned to Guaymas and established a partnership to promote and sell the holdings.

Because of his previous failure, Sam had not written to Alex for some time. In Guaymas, he resided at the hacienda of the Widow Carmen de Llaguna, who operated a small boarding house with her daughter Rosita. Sam was attracted to the daughter and their companionship ripened into marriage, which was performed in Tucson, Arizona, sometime during 1882.

Sam hadn't even shared the news of his marriage with Alex, other than asking that certain feminine items be sent him. When Alex queried Sam, he finally revealed the marriage and Alex sent a small gift, some money and the sage counsel that Sam might well abandon his dreams of empire and come home to the rewarding comforts of a fireplace. After all, Sam was more than sixty years old and at an age when he should be thinking of settling down. He accepted the gifts but laughingly rejected the advice.

". . . She is a fine girl and takes good care of me," Sam wrote later. "We are presently poor but happy. Please address me as Señor del Brannan, as that is the name the Mexicans insist upon using . . . I like it somehow."

Despite his age and a constitution which had been eroded with the effects of the old gunshot wounds and years of intemperate living, he wrote again on August 12, 1882:

". . . I am leaving to go into the interior to inspect my property, even though my wife argues against it . . ." He did admit to a lame arm and some other general infirmities, but he remembered to order a long list of needed supplies, which included an old letter press which he had stored in San Francisco many years before. He wanted to print some circulars and other materials for his promotion.

Alex was especially pleased when Sam asked that a large painting of himself be shipped with the rest of the items. Alex believed that it indicated a new grip on life, a renewed joy of living, but Alex had to cinch his financial belt a bit to comply with all of the requests, for Sam still did not know that there was nothing left from the wreckage of his estate.

Sam didn't write for a long time after that. He was too shaken with the desertion of his wife, who had bluntly told him that she didn't want to continue their marriage since his land claim apparently wasn't going to come to anything. He had to swallow his pride as he finally wrote of the dissolution of this third marriage.

He complained now about the returning numbness and paralysis in his left side, which the Calistoga doctor predicted he might suffer as a result of the gunshot wounds. His friend John Ricketson wanted to hospitalize Sam but he firmly rejected the offer, even when Ricketson offered to pay for the care. He couldn't stand the thought of being caged and left to die in a hospital. It wasn't that he was afraid of dying but he wanted to be free as he had always been. Ricketson had made Sam's life as easy as possible by making him a partner in the real estate business, a duty which didn't really require much effort. But the thought of death continued to plague Sam. At length he made a decision. He shaved carefully, put on his best clothes and went to call on Adam Willard, who was the United States consul at Guaymas.

"Welcome, Mr. Brannan, I've heard of you," Willard said. "I know much of your work in California."

Brannan smiled and thanked the consul. He was pleased to know his fame was not as transient as it might have seemed.

"How may I help you?"

Sam reached inside his coat and extracted a sheet of paper. It was covered with a scrawl, showing a hand which wavered with the weight of age and impairment. "I would like to have this document formally witnessed," Sam said. "It is my will." Consul Willard nodded and called two other consul employees, John Wilson and John Young, to witness that Sam Brannan had signed the document which said:

"In the name of God, Amen. I declare all former wills null and void this day, July 24, 1883.

"I bequeath and give to my son, Samuel Brannan, Jr., one dollar, and to my eldest daughter, Adelaide, one dollar; and to my third and youngest daughter, Lizzie Brannan, one dollar.

"The reason that I bequeath so small a sum is that I gave their mother at the time of our divorce a large fortune of more than a half million dollars and she took charge of the children and alienated them from me and I have learned that she has squandered it away to gambling and mining stocks, which I am sorry to hear."

"And I give and bequeath to John Ricketson, now residing in Guaymas, Mexico, one half of all my property in New Guaymas on Point Arena, Block 9.

"My nephew, the oldest son of my sister, Mary Ann Badlam, now residing in San Francisco, to share and share alike in one half of each of my 10 Mexican claims of land and railroad franchises or money. Ricketson paying one half of the land cost to me in New Guaymas, Eight hundred ($800) Dollars.

"They, Ricketson and Badlam, paying all of my honest debts and my funeral expenses to be levied on my property in Block One, New Guaymas, Mexico, they are to prosecute all those claims against Mexico not paid.

Sam'l Brannan"

Alex, Ricketson and The Sacramento *Union* were all provided copies of the document. It seemed that Sam had finally thrown in the sponge, a victim of adverse and cruel fates.

But it was not to be.

The Mexican government dangled another prize of 200,-000 acres situated on the Tagin River, then withdrew it when Sam didn't have enough money to survey it, let alone develop the land as they required. Both Alex and Ricketson made secret overtures to the San Francisco Odd Fellows Lodge, asking for a pension for its founder and certainly most illustrious member, who had always contributed heavily to the lodge while he was able. Sam wasn't told of their efforts, because pride would never have permitted him to accept such money if he had known.

Other efforts were made for him, most of which amounted to very little. Unfortunately for Sam, he had become a legend during his own lifetime. San Franciscans spoke of his doings as though he were already dead, and they didn't thank anyone for reminding them that he was still alive and could be helped as he once had helped so many others. Many of those who turned their backs were people who had profited when Sam's empire collapsed and they gobbled up his properties at cut-rate prices.

But Sam still had a surprise for them all. He wasn't dead. Far from it. He wrote Alex and Ricketson when he arrived in Nogales, Arizona, and soon he announced a new location written on a letterhead which proclaimed:

Sam Brannan
Dealer in Real Estate of All Kinds
Escondido, California

20 End of the Dream

"I've decided to start all over again," Sam wrote to Alex in a laborious scrawl. "This is a new area, and there is great opportunity even for one with limited capital." He thought a moment, then added that his health was much improved and even extended an invitation for Alex to visit him at his new home.

Alex did. After arriving in San Diego, California, in November, 1888, Alex rode a few miles inland to the delightful, sun-drenched vale in which Escondido was situated. Alex smiled as he noticed the posters pinned to the trees which advertised the services of Sam'l Brannan, Esquire, as a real estate agent.

"The Mexicans named this village properly," Alex laughed after they had exchanged greetings. "Name means the 'hide-away,' doesn't it?"

"Sí, señor," Sam replied facetiously. "But don't you think I am going to hide my talents," he pointed to the brave posters. But for all his laughter, the years hadn't been kind to Sam, who now made his way about with a painful and obvious limp. But his eyes were bright and his mind seemed as keen as ever as it leaped from one new plan to another.

Sam bombarded Alex with questions about San Francisco and his old friends. He explained his unfortunate marriage in Mexico, even defending his ex-wife's actions. "She was understandably disappointed when my promises of wealth and security dissolved," Sam said quietly. "She was a fine woman and would be much better off to make up the rest of her life with a younger man."

Sam explained that he now made his home with a fine, kind lady named Magdalena Moraga who looked after him as she would a member of her own family.

Sam wanted Alex to see the property which he called his "ranch," but first they went to his room to clean up. It was a large, windowed room. While the furnishings were sparse, the furniture was heavy and hand-carved, which fitted the decor of the heavy-beamed room on the second floor. Sam walked to a small table which stood beneath a wide window. Beside a small bouquet of freshly picked flowers was placed a small decanter, blood red because of its contents.

"Would you care for a glass of wine?" he asked, pointing to the container. Alex nodded, and Sam filled one glass with wine and a second glass with spring water.

"You're not having any?" Alex asked in surprise.

Sam laughed. "Don't look so amazed. I've drunk enough for one lifetime. I've given it up now. Without drinking I will be in a better position to seize on whatever opportunities I have left to me."

Alex smiled and patted Sam's shoulder affectionately. They went downstairs and out of the building, their arms linked.

They walked a short distance to where Sam pointed out about one hundred acres of neatly tended fig trees. "These'll be worth a fortune one day soon, but now they take care and time."

There was something about Sam's new attitude that

pleased Alex, and he was glad that he had made the trip to see him. Though he didn't share the thought with Sam, Alex went away determined to get help for his uncle from the Odd Fellows Lodge. His concern was rewarded by news from the Lodge that a pension had been established for Sam. The Lodge officials softened the pension's implied charity with a formal letter stating that it was a customary procedure and represented official Lodge recognition of meritorious service on the part of charter members, of which Sam Brannan was number one. Sam seemed satisfied with the explanation and accepted the pension gratefully.

Sam's continued faith in his future seemed confirmed when he received a letter from H. H. Bancroft, noted California historian, asking him to write his memoirs to be included in Bancroft's monumental and definitive history of the West. Flattered, Sam scrawled a note accepting the assignment and in his usual grand manner told Bancroft that he could pay him whatever he considered the work to be worth.

"After all," Brannan wrote with a touch of the old bravado, "I am independent and have no immediate need for money . . ." Sam liked that touch, and while he felt in a grandiloquent mood he also wrote a letter to Alex advising that the regular check from his properties need not be sent because of the pension and the prospect of a substantial sum from Bancroft. "Perhaps an accounting every quarter," Sam said, "would serve the purpose.

"Besides all this, Mr. Dowd, a lawyer of international fame, is actively pressing my Mexican claims and that would be a substantial windfall, as you know.

"Life is good and the future again seems bright," Sam added confidentially. "I am working on my memoirs and believe that they will add a new dimension to the real history of California when they are completed."

But Sam had to set aside his letter-writing for a time.

Lands sales became brisk, his fig trees needed attention and he wanted to give more thought to the memoirs. Sam realized that a capsule sketch of his entire life wasn't easily contrived. He had pondered the subject for so long after lunch that he slipped into a siesta, his feet propped up on the porch railing, his straw hat slouched down over his eyes. But he popped awake as a messenger from the post office shook him. The youth handed him a registered letter from Mexico City with the official seal of the Mexican government.

"Ah, what's this?" Sam asked as he shook the sleep from his mind. He signed, then ran a finger beneath the flap and pushed open the envelope. Along with a folded letter, a long piece of paper fluttered to the ground. Sam let it lie as he read the letter. His eyes widened as he scanned the lines, then he suddenly stopped and grabbed up the piece of paper.

"A check. A check for forty-nine thousand dollars!" he cried, his voice cracking with emotion. He slumped back into his chair, weak with emotion. He looked at the check, then reread the letter conveying the money.

The Mexican government had finally recognized the obligation it owed to him for his extraordinary services in behalf of Mexico. Noting that the previous land grants hadn't proved a fair settlement, they were offering the enclosed check in full settlement of all claims present and future in hopes he would accept it and enable them to close the matter.

Sam had a wild impulse to yell "yes, yes!" before he realized that all he had to do was to sign and return the attached voucher, indicating his release, and the check would be honored at the San Diego banks.

Despite his happiness, Sam was able to keep the mammoth secret until he had cash in hand. He didn't want to be embarrassed by having credit refused when he went to buy new clothes. He didn't buy extravagantly but chose clothes he thought would be in keeping for a man nearly seventy years old. Seventy, yes, but a man of affluence and one accustomed to wealth. He dressed carefully and had his gray beard trimmed, the sideburns clipped and his cheeks closely shaved and powdered. Once fully dressed, it was hard to resist the temptation to turn into a tavern, throw a handful of gold coins on the bar and order drinks for everyone.

But Sam checked the impulse. He knew if he resumed the role, he wouldn't stop until the money was gone, and there were more important things to tend to. As Sam turned that phrase over in his mind, he thought it quite unlike the Sam Brannan of the old days.

But he did indulge in one whimsy when he paid his landlady, Mrs. Moraga, a handsome bonus for all of the extra care she had provided him over the years. He tended to his few affairs, then took a ship to San Francisco, with nearly every cent of the $49,000 with him.

In San Francisco, Sam burst into Alex's office, taking his nephew by surprise. Sam hadn't written because what he had in mind had to be explained in person.

After greeting Alex, he asked him to dig out all of the old account books and to total any debts that might have been left unpaid.

When Alex protested that it would mean a lot of unnecessary work, Sam was ready. Dramatically he flung the money belt on Alex's desk. "There she is. Nearly forty-nine thousand dollars," Sam said, his voice choked with emotion. "I want all of my debts paid, as far as she'll go."

Alex said he didn't think that it would cover all of the debts, but by compromising the debts and paying the same percentage to all, it would stretch. Sam nodded that would be fair.

He did hold out just a trifle to indulge himself in some final memories of past days of glory. He wandered about San Francisco seeking out old friends, at least those who still remembered that he was still alive. Sam was expansive. Briefly once again he was living. He explained that he was dabbling in real estate and ranching near San Diego, and had settled a Mexican deal which he was devoting to the payment of some trifling obligations in San Franicsco.

It was a grand reunion for Sam and he felt restored when it was all over and he was again on his way back to Escondido. He seemed to walk without a limp, his face glowed with health, and his cocky smile had returned. Before leaving Alex, he embraced the younger man.

"You'll be hearing from me, Alex," Sam said, his face crinkled in smiles. "There are great days ahead for all of us."

Sam didn't even flinch when he returned to Escondido to find that his memoirs had been destroyed in a fire and that he would have to start them all over again. He would have to work harder than ever now. Time was shorter, and there was no money. But Sam was happier than he had been for a long time. He had settled all of his debts; he owed no one.

Once back in Escondido, he slipped out of his fine clothes and gave them to Mrs. Moraga with the comment they were to be used "for burying purposes," then took a deep breath and picked up life as it had been.

But not for long. Sam Brannan died of the infirmities of age on May 5, 1889, his seventieth year. Even then his story was not finished.

For some unexplained reason, no one was notified of his death, and after simple services, with Mrs. Moraga as his only mourner, his body lay in the public receiving vault for sixteen months until some public official finally located Alex. He was sent a bill for the rental of the public crypt and the final expenses. The bill, for thirty-one dollars, was paid on October 1, 1890. Sam was then buried in the Mt. Hope Cemetery, San Diego. For thirty years, his grave was marked only with a small redwood stake. Then an admirer and friend of the Brannan family, J. Harvey McCarthy, purchased a dignified granite monument upon which he had inscribed these words:

Sam Brannan
1819.................1889
California Pioneer of '46
Dreamer—Leader
and
Empire Builder

Few men deserved such praise more.

Bibliography

Bailey, Paul. *Sam Brannan and The California Mormons.* Los Angeles: Westernlore Press, 1959.

Coblentz, Stanton. *Villains and Vigilantes.* New York: Thomas Yoseloff, Inc., 1957.

Davis, William Heath. *Seventy-Five Years in California.* San Francisco: John Howell, 1929.

Johnson, Kenneth (ed.). *San Francisco As It Was. Gleanings from the Picayune.* Georgetown, California: The Talisman Press, 1964.

Lewis, Oscar. *This Was San Francisco.* New York: David McKay, 1962.

O'Dea, Thomas F. *The Mormons.* Chicago: Phoenix Press, 1964.

Rogers, Fred Blackburn (ed.). *The California Star, Yerba Buena and San Francisco.* (Vol. I, 1847-1848.) Berkeley, California: Howell-North Books, 1965.

Scherer, James A. *The First Forty-Niner.* New York: Minton-Balch, 1925.

Scott, Reva. *Samuel Brannan and the Golden Fleece.* New York: Macmillan, 1944.

Stellman, Louis. *Sam Brannan, Builder of San Francisco.* New York: Exposition Press, 1953.

Stewart, George R. *Committee of Vigilance, Revolution in San Francisco, 1851.* Boston: Houghton-Mifflin, 1964.

Valentine, Alan. *Vigilante Justice.* New York: Reynal & Co., 1956.

Index

About the Author

The collaboration of Bob and Jan Young had its beginnings at the University of California at Los Angeles (UCLA) where they met as undergraduates and shared a common interest in writing. Following their marriage in 1940, they spent most of the next ten years in the weekly newspaper field, with the exception of two years Bob served in the Army during World War II.

In 1950 they left the newspaper field for freelance writing, concentrating on the magazine field. In 1958 they expanded their writing interests still further with the publication of their first book for young people. Since then they have used their collaboration to author a wide range of books, including fiction, non-fiction and biography. Today they consider writing for young people their major interest though they still remain active in the magazine field.

Both are native Californians. Bob was born November 6, 1916, in Chico, attended Sacramento schools, UCLA and graduated from the University of Nevada. Jan was born March 6, 1919, in Lancaster, attended San Diego and South Pasadena public schools and UCLA. They have four children: Michael, a civil engineer; Tim, a professional baseball player; Gary, currently serving in the Army Engineers; and Randi, a student.